God Has Purposed Your Child

21ST CENTURY GUIDANCE FOR DISCOVERING YOUR CHILD'S PURPOSE

God Has Purposed Your Child

21ST CENTURY GUIDANCE FOR DISCOVERING YOUR CHILD'S PURPOSE

by
Patricia Flanagan Stanek

Copyright © 2017 Patricia Flanagan Stanek
All rights reserved. No part of this book may be used or reproduced in any manner whatsoever without prior written consent of the authors, except as provided by the United States of America copyright law.

Published by Best Seller Publishing®, Pasadena, CA
Best Seller Publishing® is a registered trademark
Printed in the United States of America.
ISBN 978-1-946978-27-1

This publication is designed to provide accurate and authoritative information with regard to the subject matter covered. It is sold with the understanding that the publisher is not engaged in rendering legal, accounting, or other professional advice. If legal advice or other expert assistance is required, the services of a competent professional should be sought. The opinions expressed by the authors in this book are not endorsed by Best Seller Publishing® and are the sole responsibility of the author rendering the opinion.

Most Best Seller Publishing® titles are available at special quantity discounts for bulk purchases for sales promotions, premiums, fundraising, and educational use. Special versions or book excerpts can also be created to fit specific needs.

For more information, please write:
Best Seller Publishing®
1346 Walnut Street, #205
Pasadena, CA 91106
or call 1(626) 765 9750
Toll Free: 1(844) 850-3500
Visit us online at: www.BestSellerPublishing.org

Foreword

By
Renne Cole Dowler

What does any parent want for their child? To be of God and have a successful life. This book is a must read for any parent preparing their child for the future. This book is a wealth of information on options that are available for a path to establishing a career. Patricia's insight through a Biblical and practical application to determine a child's purpose in life is much needed in society today as so many children are being educated outside of their God given talents. This is not just a book of facts, but a well-researched book of guidance rooted in God's Word.

I have personally known Patricia since our children were very small. She is a dedicated and loving mother who is preparing for her own child's future. She is a dear friend and sister in Christ that has walked with me through the triumphs and the most difficult times in my life without ever wavering in her strength and tenacity. She is a knowledgeable and caring teacher as this book will illustrate the depth of her research and experience. Above and beyond anything else, her love and devotion for the Lord and being of service to Him is the central part of who she is as a person.

As I watched Patricia prepare for this book, I witnessed firsthand how much she wanted her work to be of value for everyone preparing for the future of their children with guidance from God. My fervent prayer is that this book will be read by many and bless all that read it.

Table of Contents

I. First Things First 1
    A. God's Requirement to Discover His Plan
       and Purpose 1
    B. Parents .... This is for You! 4
    C. Moving Forward 6

II. Assessment of Personal Gifts 9
    A. Assessing......Why is it so valuable? 9
    B. How Schools Can Help Our Children
       Discover Their Personal Gifts 13
    C. What are Spiritual Gifts? 19

III. Why Finding Your Purpose is So Important? .. 23
    A. Communing with God to Discover His
       Plan and Purpose 23
    B. Purpose as it Relates to Work 26
    C. Correlation between Assessments and
       Being Happy at Work 28

IV. Assessments at Different Stages of
    Development 33
    A. Assessments during Middle School and
       High School 33
    B. Assessments during College, Technical
       School, or Military Enlistment 35
    C. Assessments When Entering the Workforce 37

V.	What About the "Gap Year"?	43
	A. Out of School Youth	43
	B. "Gap Year" …..Getting More Attention	45
	C. What is Career Maturity?	47
	D. Possible Outcomes of Taking the "Gap Year"	49
VI.	Hindrances to Finding God's Plan and Purpose	53
	A. Disobedience	53
	B. Lack of Self Reflection and Discernment	55
	C. Worldly Interventions – Drugs, Alcohol, Bad Influences	59
	D. Poor Decisions	60
	E. Getting Into Debt	61
VII.	Developing a Career Path to begin a Journey	65
	A. Career Planning and When to Start	65
	B. Tools to Use: Informational Interviews, Job Shadows, Mentoring	69
	C. Interview Colleges, instead of them Interviewing You	72
	1. Career Centers on College Campuses	75
	D. Success in College……What it Takes to Get the Degree	76

Table of Contents

VIII.	What Paths to Pursue Your Purpose	79
	A. Career/Technical Education While in High School	80
	B. College or University	84
	C. Technical College	88
	D. Military Branch	90
	E. Online Degrees	91
	F. Apprenticeships.... Earn While You Learn	95
	G. Entering the Workforce after High School	97
IX.	Our World Needs People with Technical Skills…….. Is this a Path for You to find Your Purpose?	99
	A. Coding Skills as Part of the Core Curriculum?	99
	B. Benefits of Teaching Coding Skills as Part of the Core Curriculum	102
	C. What Coding Skills Can Offer a Student	104
	D. Technology Proliferates	107
X.	Career Paths in the 21st Century	109
	A. Career Clusters – A Starting Place for Students	109
	B. Career and Technical Education on the Rise	112
	C. 21st Century Labor Market — What are Employers Seeking?	115

XI. People Skills/Soft Skills....God Wants Us To Relate Well with One Another 121
    A. Why People Skills/Soft Skills are Necessary for a Student to Succeed 121
    B. Social Media: Being Appropriate 125
    C. Develop Yourself (Graciously).................... 126
    D. Teens Need Nurturing, Too! 129

XII. When a Child Knows His or Her Purpose 133
    A. The Advantaged Life.. 133
    B. <u>Personality Types:</u> Why Knowing Your Type Can Provide Insight 134
    C. What God Wants for You........................... 137
        1. Jeremiah 29:11 (Bible Quote for Students)

"For I know the plans I have for you, declares the Lord, plans to prosper you and not to harm you, plans to give you hope and a future."

Proverbs 22:6 (Bible Quote for Parents)

"Train up a child in the way he should go (according to his bent), And even when he is old he will not depart from it."

    D. Concluding Thoughts 138

All Scripture References in this book are from the New International Version

Endorsements

I am so impressed with this book. It will definitely minister to this culture and underachieving generation. As I travel across this country I watch, I observe and I listen to what's being said to this generation.

Trish has written eloquently page after page to this (culture) generation. It's inspiring, powerful and life-changing. I was really engaged on two chapters. Chapter 2 "Gifts" is great for growing children. I found Chapter 6 very intriguing on Hindrances to Finding God's Plan and Purpose. Three major points: Disobedience, Lack of Self Confidence and Poor Decisions. Wow, what insight!

This is not just a book with wonderful principles, but a map or compass on how to raise this next generation.

Randy DonGiovanni
RandyDon Ministries
Youth Specialist

As a mother of two adult sons, a middle school teacher, and one who is involved in the lives of many young people, I find this book to be a wonderful tool. Truly when a young person knows who he or she is in Christ and has the assurance that the gifts God has given to him or her will be used for His Kingdom, the possibilities are endless. As you read the pages of this excellent handbook for the future, be encouraged that God has a great plan for your life.

Glenna Carter
Middle School Teacher
Central Christian Academy

....

With so many children entering early adulthood unsure of their specific purpose, this book is a much needed tool. Patricia wonderfully ties together God's truths, a child's unique design, and a clear plan that is sure to have positive results. As a father of four, and pastor, I will use this book as a resource for years to come.

Kurt Jenkins
Lead Pastor
Central Assembly of God

Endorsements

Today's youth are being bombarded with unrealistic expectations of what it takes to be successful. Many are afraid to take that "leap of faith" and pursue their purpose and passion because their principles are not rooted in the Love and Faith of Jesus Christ. This book is an excellent guide for parents and students alike to understanding how to prepare for the future according to God's plan. It is a well thought out guide to believing and trusting in what the Lord has purposed for our children. Trish is passionate about her Faith in the Lord as well as helping students to recognize the gifts that have been bestowed upon them by the Heavenly Father. Her belief in preparing young people according to God's Purpose for their lives is illuminated in the chapters of this book.

Shelley Sowers
High School Teacher
Bethlehem-Center High School

God Has Purposed Your Child is a great read for both High School/post school kids and their parents. I love the tips and ideas of how to ready your child for their career and life. My favorite personal tip was developing a daily quote to speak over his or her life. A couple other critical topics are assessments and the development of your soft skills, both are critical when positioning yourself for success after High School. As our company stays on the lookout for talent, understanding those assessments and seeing those soft skills in action put you in a class above. I highly recommend this book!

Anthony D. Brock
VP of Finance Lighthouse Electric Co., Inc.

Dedication

This book is dedicated to honor the memory of these Beautiful, Godly Women:

Faith Renne' Dowler

Rhoda Malone

Breanna Africa

Trust in the LORD with all your heart
and lean not on your own understanding;
in all your ways submit to him,
and he will make your paths straight.

Proverbs 3:5-6

About the Author

Patricia Flanagan Stanek is a high school teacher in Washington County, Pennsylvania. She supervises a career awareness organization for the students in her school. She is certified in Business, Computer, Information Technology and Cooperative Education. Trish's educational background is a Master of Science in Human Resource Development from Florida International University and a Bachelor of Science in Business Administration from Robert Morris University. Trish recently obtained a Biz Innovator Certification from an online program with the University of Iowa, Jacobson Institute of Youth Entrepreneurship. She was formerly contracted to the Employment and Training Administration, U.S. Department of Labor.

She teaches 21st Century Computer Applications, Accounting, Coding Skills, Entrepreneurship, and Exploring Career Paths Classes. Trish has coordinated eight college/career fairs at her school as a project for the career awareness organization. She teaches her students the value of conducting informational interviews and job shadow experiences in preparation for selecting post-secondary career paths. She helps students understand the importance of networking skills. She has knowledge of the labor market to assist students in choosing career paths that will offer opportunities and career advancement.

Trish is a member of Central Assembly of God Church in Houston, PA and is married to her husband, John and has a daughter, Sarah, who will enter college in the fall of 2018.

Chapter I
First Things First

God's Requirement to Discover His Plan and Purpose

Yes, GOD has purposed your child to accomplish, achieve, and attain specific things that only they can accomplish, achieve, and attain. Your child was not born to just attend our K-12 school system, go to college or technical school, get a job, live their life, and then die. God's Plan and Purpose for your child is much bigger than that.

Did you know that your child, your gift sent from Heaven was created for signs and wonders, miracles and testimonies, blessings and power? Imagine that! Parents are the primary influence to help a child discover what God created them to do.

> *However, as it is written: "What no eye has seen, what no ear has heard, and what no human mind has conceived"*
> *—the things God has prepared for those who love him—*
> I Corinthians 2:9

He wants you to know that your child was created for things that you cannot dream of on your own. These things are to do the impossible and accomplish their own individual purpose God has set aside just for them. This purpose is not a light one. It is vital to this world for your child to take their position through seeking God's beautiful, wondrous plan and path for their life.

To find purpose, the first thing God requires us to do is to receive His Son, Jesus, as personal Lord and Savior. Jesus came to earth to do what we cannot do for ourselves. By receiving the redemptive atonement for our sins when Jesus died on Calvary's Cross; it allows us to be accepted by God. It is as easy as **ABC!** Allow me to explain: **Admitting** we are sinners, **Believing** in Jesus that His Death and Resurrection paid the penalty for our sins, and **Confessing** Jesus as Lord and Savior. Once we receive this free gift of salvation, we can seek God's Plan and Purpose for our lives because we are now His Children. Prior to receiving Jesus as Lord and Savior, a person is separated from God due to their sins.

To become a child of God, it is not something a person can earn or work toward. That is a difficult thing for some people to understand, but according to the Bible, that is the "Gospel Truth". We are **NOT** saved by our works, morality, religion, or anything else **WE** can do.

> *Jesus replied, "Very truly I tell you, no one can see the Kingdom of God unless they are born again."*
> *John 3:3*

What God thinks about "our works":

> *All of us have become like one who is unclean, and all our righteous acts are like filthy rags; we all shrivel up like a leaf, and like the wind our sins sweep us away.*
> *Isaiah 64:6*

Jesus is referring to being born the second time of the spirit, not of the flesh. He was having a conversation with the Pharisee, Nicodemus, to explain how to enter the Kingdom of God. Nicodemus did not understand what Jesus meant "to be born again".

> *Flesh gives birth to flesh, but the spirit*
> *gives birth to spirit.*
>
> *John 3:6*

PARENTS…..THIS IS FOR YOU!

A child is never an accident, no matter the circumstances of their birth. God does not make mistakes. We must always remember that! All of the attributes that make your child who they are ….. such as personality, temperament, values, interests, skills, strengths, aptitudes, and so on, are not to be found…..in this combination….in any one else…..JUST Your Child! That's how special each child is to God! Please know this and take hold of it. Of course, we can come to this realization at any age in our lives.

Take a moment with me to imagine the life of a person who realizes, when they are a small child, that God has created them for a specific purpose. How amazing could that person's life be if they acknowledged this realization early in life?

I. First Things First

How incredible is that? Your child's uniqueness is nothing short of God's Design. There has never been or ever will be someone just like them……even if they are an identical twin! Even identical twins are different from one another. Every child is born equipped by God no matter their intelligence level. Parents of gifted, typical, and special needs children please know that you are God's Partner in harvesting the God-Given "personal" and spiritual gifts in your children.

> *Children are a heritage from the LORD,*
> *offspring a reward from him.*
> *Like arrows in the hands of a warrior*
> *are children born in one's youth.*
> **Psalm 127:3-4**

Therefore, after a person receives Jesus, then they can begin to seek God every day so that God may reveal His awesome Plan and Purpose. Always remember that pursuing God's Plan and Purpose for your life will be an amazing adventure. You will have divine protection and provision accompanying you wherever you go! That is hard for the human mind to grasp, but that is true. Who would not want God's Protection and Provision?

Moving Forward

*The tongue has the power of life and death,
and those who love it will eat its fruit.*
Proverbs 18:21

This being true, help your child to develop a daily quote to speak over their life.

Something like this....

> "I am a confident, hardworking, young person who will achieve, accomplish, and attain great things in my life because God has a great plan and purpose for my life."

Your words are powerful to bring your faith to life. As your child develops the habit of speaking life regarding what God has in store for them, the child will become what they speak. I actually recommend "speaking over one's life" to begin earlier than the teen years because it will help to combat the potential problems that may accompany adolescence. Many teens face battles in their minds. This is evident with the large number of teens who are depressed, filled with anxiety, lack confidence, are being bullied, and too often commit suicide. All of these negative experiences could be avoided if only our teens were aware of who God is, what God has already done for them, and what God has planned and purposed for their lives. The enemy of their souls has used one of his tools, "deception", to cause havoc on some teens in this generation. It is time for us to interrupt the enemy's plan for this generation. It is written in:

> *The thief comes only to steal and kill and*
> *destroy; I have come that they may have*
> *life, and have it to the full.*
> *John 10:10*

Jesus wants us to have life and live it to the fullest. It is time for our teens to know and understand they are valuable, unique, and special to God. They need to know that they have much to contribute to their families, their communities, the economy they live in, and to fulfill God's Mission for their lives.

> *Consecrate yourselves, for tomorrow the*
> *Lord will do amazing things among you.*
> *Joshua 3:5*

When a person sets himself apart for the Lord and knows their "personal" and spiritual gifts to fulfill their calling, that's the kind of life that we were all meant to live. Parents are a crucial component in teaching their children to set themselves apart to fulfill God's Plan and Purpose in their lives. This is a very intentional act.

Chapter II
Assessment of Personal Gifts

Assessing....Why is it so Valuable?

As I began to write this chapter, I was thinking of an acronym for the word "gifts". One evening, it came to me. God programs children in the womb so these things are in our children when they are born:

"G"od's "I"nstruction "F"or "T"alents "S"trengths
→ GIFTS ←

As a child grows up, parents observe qualities in their child. Is the child quiet or boisterous; outgoing or reserved; a follower or a natural-born leader; creative or lacks creativity; an extrovert or an introvert; athletic or artistic? Whatever the unique qualities are in the child, parents can catalog those qualities to help their child begin to seek God's Plan and Purpose for their life. God has deposited and programmed gifts into each child. A parent can do one of two things with those gifts: Help discover them, foster them, and nurture them or try to develop gifts that they want the child to have (that are not evidently present in the child). I strongly advise parents to foster and nurture the "personal gifts" in the child because both parties will benefit from this avenue.

In his book, *The Untapped Power of Praise*, Kenneth Hagin, Jr., writes: "Obtaining the Full Measure of God's Blessing." He writes about how we all have gifts:

> "There are other areas where we probably all need to experience increase in our lives. For example, each one of us has dreams, desires, gifts, and talents placed inside of us by God. But many of us don't know how to develop our gifts or how to use our talents productively to the glory of God. Many of us have dreams, but we don't know how to practically implement those dreams so they become a reality in our lives" (Hagin 105).

I would agree that many people do not discover or harness their gifts early in life and sometimes not at all. What a waste of God's Gifting!

These "personal gifts" are being developed as children attend elementary, middle, and high school.

II. Assessment of Personal Gifts

Parents, teachers, counselors, mentors, and youth ministers can all play a role in helping children identify and harvest the gifts God has deposited in them. Some gifts are more visible and evident than others, but a child most definitely has gifts that can and should be used to develop God's Plan and Purpose for their life and to seek college/career opportunities that will benefit the child.

Having knowledge of these "personal gifts" is valuable because when a student knows their gifts they will migrate toward opportunities that allow those "personal gifts" to be developed. How exciting is that? Humans, by nature, want to excel. It is at the core of our being. No human being wakes up in the morning and says, "I want to fail today!" We are not built like that. Even in their earliest attempts, children seek success and approval. God wants us to succeed in everything we do. God also wants us to seek Him in all we do. Conversely, the enemy of our souls wants us to fail in all we do.

Every fall when I start a new school year, I go over the rules and responsibilities of being a student in my classroom. I also let the students know that I want them to succeed in everything they do in my classroom and I want them to succeed in life. That's why I use time during the school year to allow them to participate in some online and paper assessment tools to gather data on themselves. I believe the students will achieve more if they know more about who they are. It makes them feel good about who they are.

For instance, Marcus Buckingham in the "Trombone Player Wanted" (Buckingham) speaks about his four-year old son. Marcus says, "his son is very competitive, likes structure"(Buckingham). What is interesting about this observation is that Marcus goes on to say that those qualities "ain't going to change over his son's lifespan."(Buckingham) I agree. Why do we think we have to wait until our children are going off to college or coming out of college to discover these personal attributes? The attributes have been deposited in the child long before the child decides on a college major or career choice. Why do we wait until a child is declaring a major for them to "figure themselves out"? I have spoken to many college admissions counselors that have said that "undecided" is the #1 college major. I believe the reason for that is because students have not properly "assessed themselves" or participated in any assessment activities prior to their entry into our college and university campuses. I would even venture to say that most students (high school and college) have not sought God's Plan and Purpose for their lives. May I suggest to this generation of students that instead of "trying to find yourself" at the expense of a college education, find out who God is and seek His Plan for your life which will far exceed you "trying to find yourself"?

How Schools Can Help Our Children Discover Their Personal Gifts

Our school systems are focused on developing student's academic abilities and achievements. I understand that is the primary objective of K-12 Education. However, should we consider having our teachers and parents (beginning in Kindergarten) work together to identify the personal gifts, talents, personalities, and abilities in our students and continue collecting data on the students all the way through the K-12 experience? What an amazing collection of information on an individual that would be; even if there was just a short paragraph written by one teacher for each grade along the way and kept in a database. This database could be used by the student, their parents, and their guidance counselor when creating a college/career plan and ultimately pursuing God's Plan and Purpose. What possibilities could be unveiled? This information would be invaluable for the student and their parents along with the student's academic record to align and predict post-secondary opportunities for success. What a collection of a child's developmental process!

Our schools are consumed with reaching academic benchmarks and getting students to pass standardized tests. We tend to "pigeon hole" all students into reaching certain academic standards at certain times throughout their academic K-12 experience. I would like to challenge our school systems to realize that the 21st Century is very different from the 20th Century. We should be trying to implement more individualized and customized learning opportunities that seek to bring out the "personal gifts" in our students. I believe we would get better academic results because students who participate in learning opportunities that appeal to them are motivated to achieve. I am a strong believer in project-based learning. These are experiential in nature and give students opportunities to work in teams, collaborate, communicate, problem solve, resolve conflict, and produce results. All of these skills are in demand in the 21st Century Workforce so why shouldn't our schools be directing instruction toward the development of these abilities in all students? I am sure these things are being taught, on some level, in our schools, but should be the norm, not the occasional supplemental activity.

A student's personal attributes are mostly a mystery even to the student as they work their way through our

II. Assessment of Personal Gifts

high schools. I have worked with high school students who are excited to take a personality test while in a class. They discover much about themselves that gives them information about who they are. Another observation I have made is that when the students participate in these types of assessments (such as personality tests, interest inventories, value assessments, aptitude tests) their confidence and belief in themselves is displayed in their behavior afterward. They get excited about who they are! I get excited too because I know the results are all part of what God wants the student to learn about themselves.

One of the reasons I believe in assessing high school students for their "personal gifts" is because once a person gets out of high school, goes to college, starts a career, gets married, starts a family, starts paying bills (in other words becomes a responsible member of society), it is much more challenging to figure yourself out with so much more being at stake. Not to say you can't conduct assessments later in life, but I believe the optimal time in a person's lifespan to get the most of the assessment process is when a person is young. How many working adults have never been assessed for their "personal gifts"? I would venture to say that number is high!

Of course, all students are unique and mature at their own pace. So depending on the student's maturity level, assessments can be introduced in the middle school grades. I believe that it is during these grades (6th-8th) that formal assessments (personality tests, interest inventories, aptitude tests) would help the student and their parents in preparation for knowing what direction the student may be interested in pursuing once the student transitions into high school.

I have worked with many students who even in their senior year, have no idea of the direction they will pursue after high school. I understand it is difficult to make such challenging decisions at the young age of 18. However, students that have taken time to reflect, assess, and "do their homework" should be able to start on a career path. What I would say to a graduating senior is, "Do you have any thoughts about what path to pursue, any career interests, things you like to do?" From my experience, students want to learn about their "personal gifts". As someone who has worked in a classroom for most of her career, I can say that students who have some self awareness regarding their "personal gifts" are excited about using the time in high school to develop and enhance these gifts. I must admit; it is a beautiful thing to witness. When a student taps into their gifts, I believe that confidence and self assuredness are natural byproducts of the student using their gifts. I believe all of our high school students should be provided

II. Assessment of Personal Gifts

opportunities to find their "personal gifts" as part of their school experience.

Conducting assessments in 9th grade can be beneficial for determining if a student may want to pursue an interest in the Career and Technical Training Programs available through most high schools. I recently spoke with a young lady in her early 20s who works as a hair stylist who always knew she wanted to be a hair stylist. She is fantastic at her work. Not only does she provide a great haircut, she has wonderful people skills with her customers. During our conversations, she informed me that she attended Beauty School after high school and has the student loan debt to prove it. She realized as an adult that she should have attended the career and technical program offered free of charge from her high school program.

This is great insight for students who are interested in Career and Technical Programs that they can obtain free of charge while in high school. There are 720 days in high school (given a 180 day school year) and I can attest that it goes by very quickly. On day one of high school, students should be serious about academic excellence, extracurricular involvement, and career preparation. All of these experiences will help create a positive high school experience and equip students to make educated, well-informed decisions before pursuing college or career paths in route to finding God's Plan and Purpose for their lives.

Some things to consider when helping a young person discover God's Plan and Purpose will be as follows: Interests, Transferable Skills, Personality, Values, Strengths, Aptitudes, Types of People who they would like to work with, Types of Work Environments (Surroundings) they will thrive in, and Types of Work they would like to do.

Once a student has discovered all of these "personal gifts", the student can formulate a plan to move forward in high school or college toward a career path that will fulfill the "personal gifts" God has purposed.

While in high school, the earlier the student has done this work, the better. Students can plan their coursework, academic rigor, electives, or career/technical pathways. Participating in extracurricular activities and part-time jobs that align with their "personal gifts" will further develop and enhance these gifts to build confidence, skills, and abilities in young people. Having an understanding of "personal gifts" can be an asset when developing an online career portfolio. A high school student who already has an online career portfolio will be ahead of other teens who have not yet realized they need one. An online career portfolio is a great place to store .pdf files of a student's achievements, awards, certificates, etc. and

II. Assessment of Personal Gifts

learn to network with working professionals in careers that are of interest to them.

Here is a quote from a high school junior who was assessed for personal and spiritual gifts during middle school and how that experience has affected her and assisted her in planning a career:

> "I felt so sure of myself. I felt confidence in who I was meant to be. I felt my whole life was a treasure box waiting to be opened. I felt like I needed to know from God what He wanted me to do. I felt established in a direction of a career path. I was able to think beyond college to prepare for things even after college."

WHAT ARE SPIRITUAL GIFTS?

After receiving Jesus as Lord and Savior, a student can begin to discover God's Plan and Purpose for his or her life. In addition to the "personal gifts", there are Spiritual Gifts that God gives us. Spiritual Gifts are given by the Holy Spirit and each person has their own portion of spiritual gifts. Gifts (talents and qualities) are recorded in Romans 12:6-8 as the following: Prophecy, Serving, Teaching, Exhortation, Giving, Leadership, and Mercy.

Through the Power of the Holy Spirit "Spiritual" Gifts are given and are recorded in I Corinthians 12:8-10 as the following: **Word of Wisdom, Word of Knowledge, Discerning of Spirits, Gift of Faith, Working of Miracles, Gifts of Healing, Tongues, Interpretation of Tongues, and Prophecy.** The Holy Spirit gives "spiritual" gifts to people who believe that the Holy Spirit is active in the earth today.

> *I long to see you so that I may impart*
> *to you some spiritual gift to make*
> *you strong.*
> *Romans 1:11*

Unfortunately, some believers do not believe that the Holy Spirit is moving today. I have witnessed students who have identified these two different types of gifts and I have witnessed students who have not taken time to identify these gifts. From my experience, I have to say the students who took the time to assess their "personal" and spiritual gifts benefit greatly in pursuing their career/college plans. Unfortunately, too many students have not had the chance to assess either their "personal gifts" or their spiritual gifts. What an injustice! These are the young adults who are subject to going to college without direction, start a job just to make money, do "nothing"

II. Assessment of Personal Gifts

but sit on their parent's couch, get involved in addiction, and watch their lives diminish. Young people who know their gifts will desire to participate in opportunities to bring out their gifts. It is a natural process. Too many young people in this generation are not grasping what God has planned and purposed for them because of their rebellion or ignorance. It doesn't have to be that way. God has given them many gifts that are to be discovered, developed, enhanced, and utilized to benefit society and to glorify God on the earth.

Chapter III
Why Finding Your Purpose is So Important?

Communing with God to Discover His Plan and Purpose

God wants your child to know and understand the "personal gifts" inside of them. If they understand their "personal gifts", this knowledge and understanding can benefit them, benefit society, and glorify God. Once there is a relationship with God, a person can fully depend on what God has in store for their future. Please believe me, God's Plan and Purpose for a person's life will far exceed anything they could imagine or plan for themselves. God wants to communicate with us. Most people think that is us shooting up a prayer and then just moving on with our day. We all know that the best communication is two way. That requires us to be listeners, not just speakers. Obviously, the Bible is the best source of communication that God has provided to us. The Bible allows us to know, hear, and learn from God. In discovering what God's Plan and Purpose is, we must seek His Word to find scriptures on guidance and direction. We must pray and wait to hear from the Lord on what He would have us to do.

Unfortunately, our problem is usually rebellion. There is rebellion in every man's heart. Rebellion comes from us wanting to do things "our way" without ever considering what God would want us to do. There are many scriptures on rebellion in the Bible.

> *Remember what it says:*
> *Today when you hear his voice,*
> *don't harden your hearts*
> *as Israel did when they rebelled.*
> *Hebrews 3:15*

Consider this scenario: a young boy believes he will grow up and become an architect because his father is an architect. However, as the boy is progressing through school he realizes he is not that good in math. He tries his best and his Dad wants him to be an architect too so the boy goes to remedial math. The father gets a math tutor to try to help his son improve his math skills. But by the time the son reaches freshmen year in college, they both realize, architecture is just not a good fit for

III. Why Finding Your Purpose is So Important?

the son. Maybe this college freshmen will find his niche in marketing or public relations because he is a dynamic communicator and has excellent people skills. It would have benefitted the student and the parent to have had an honest, "reality-based" conversation prior to college regarding the weakness in math that would hinder pursuing a career in architecture.

Now consider this scenario: a young girl demonstrates a natural ability to speak in front of people. She actually feels empowered when she has to speak in front of a group of people. She learns early how to compose herself, get an audience's attention, and deliver a message that leaves an impact. Her parents observe this strength in their daughter. As she enters high school, they encourage her to seek opportunities that will allow her to further develop, enhance, and strengthen her public speaking skills. She takes their advice and by the time she is completing high school, she is very comfortable delivering speeches and making presentations prior to entering college and the workforce where these skills will be used.

Both scenarios are hypothetical; however, both could very well be true. Whatever the "personal gifts" are within a child, it will benefit the parent, the teachers, and society as a whole to not only identify the gifts, but instruct the child to seek out opportunities to practice the gifts in a variety of environments (with their friends, in school, and extracurricular activities).

PURPOSE AS IT RELATES TO WORK

I remember when I first started assessing my daughter's gifts. She took her first personality test when she was in 6th grade just to begin to discover and learn about what made her "Her". She was really excited to see the results and we read several descriptions that helped her to understand her personality type. Once I learned her personality type, it actually helped me to guide her toward her personal strengths based on what we learned. Once she got in high school, knowing her personality type, helped her to make course selections. I remember picking up a book on the different types of personalities. When she saw it on the kitchen counter one day, she asked if she could read about her personality type. She sat on the couch, all I heard was laughing and all I saw was smiling because as she read about her personality, she could not believe how accurate the description was in relationship to her personality type. At 16 ½, I decided she could benefit from taking a *StrengthsFinder®* Assessment (Gallup). She was really excited to take her *StrengthsFinder®* Assessment (Gallup). I believe when students know these types of personal attributes about themselves it gives them valuable information regarding the direction they should pursue after high school.

Students are eager to learn about what makes them tick. It is obvious when the quarterback throws winning touchdowns every Friday night that he is gifted in athletics. Additionally, it is easy to spot the possible valedictorian candidates because of the academic excellence they display in schools.

Many of our young people today are not experiencing a "real job" until they are in college or graduating from college. When I say "a real job", I mean a job that provides a paycheck with taxes taken out, responsibilities that are given, and a schedule to be followed. I believe having a high school student work in some sort of capacity during their last semester of their senior year would greatly benefit the student and our communities. It would also help to develop a "work ethic" in students that seems to be lacking today. This "work experience" opportunity would provide many benefits. It would expose high school students to the reality of a workplace with standards, productivity requirements, the importance of a work ethic, the importance of possessing 21st Century in-demand skills and many other byproducts of "work".

CORRELATION BETWEEN ASSESSMENTS AND BEING HAPPY AT WORK

People who take time to participate in assessments early in life generally experience more career satisfaction. That just makes sense, doesn't it? Because getting to know your "personal gifts" as a young person will enable that person to gravitate toward careers to utilize the "personal gifts".

As I started working with young adults and working adults in assessment of "personal gifts", I can say that most of them, young and some even middle aged, had never participated in any form of assessment to have an understanding of their "personal gifts". Generally, when people get their assessment results they are encouraged about what the feedback says. With the working adults, it has helped them to discover new career opportunities that would be more fitting than current or previous jobs that they are currently holding or have held. With young adults (high school and college students) it has helped them to begin to create a career path or select a major that is fitting to their "personal gifts". No matter when we find the "personal gifts" that God has deposited inside of us, we can discover God's Plan and Purpose for our lives. I am a proponent of discovering these gifts early, rather than later in life. Just imagine the difference between two people: One discovers God's Purpose for his life by the time they are in middle school versus the person who is almost middle aged and discovers it. Life is meant to be lived to the fullest!

> *I will make you into a great nation.*
> *I will bless you and make you famous,*
> *and you will be a blessing to others.*
> *Genesis 12:2*

For high school and college students who are seeking direction in their lives, my hope is that they are aware of this scripture. Unfortunately, many young people do not know that the enemy of their souls has destruction planned and God has Purpose and Abundant Life planned. Every young person has this amazing choice to make. Our positions as parents, teachers, mentors, youth pastors, and other influential adults in their lives are all in place to help them discover God's Purpose. However, three other influences are in play that could lead them toward the enemy's purpose: The world, the flesh, and the devil. Of course, these factors are strong influences in a young person's life especially if the young person doesn't know the Lord. If the young person knows the Lord, these factors can still be negative influences. We all make choices that have consequences. Our sins will be accounted for and judged by the Holy God. This is why it is so critical to receive Jesus' Redemptive Work on Calvary's Cross to pay the penalty for our sins.

> *For the wages of sin is death,*
> *but the free gift of God is eternal life*
> *through Christ Jesus our Lord.*
> **Romans 6:23**

As I was conducting research for this book, I was referred to a study, "How the Rich (and Happy) Get Richer (and Happier): Relationship of Core Self Evaluations to Trajectories in Attaining Work Success" (Judge 849-863). I found it very interesting, but not surprising, that the "results indicated that higher core self-evaluations were associated with both higher initial levels of work success and steeper work success trajectories"(Judge 849-863). It makes sense that people who evaluate themselves will tend to experience more happiness and success over a lifetime than those who do not evaluate themselves.

With reference to the millions of students attending our colleges and universities, why are so many going in with an "undecided" major? My perspective is that these students have not taken time to "do their homework" on

III. Why Finding Your Purpose is So Important?

themselves. In the 21st Century, we have so many ways for students to "find their niche" before attending college. Personal Assessment Tools, informational interviews, job shadows, career research, career/technical training are just a few of these tools. The problem I see is that while they are in high school, students are so busy with academics, sports, extracurricular activities, part-time jobs, texting, and social media that they don't prioritize discovering their "personal" and spiritual gifts. The enemy of their souls does not want them to focus on discovering what God has purposed them to do. The enemy of their souls wants them to be confused, doubtful, naïve, unaware, and in debt.

With over $1 Trillion in student loan debt, I would say that many of them have been subject to the enemy's plan for their lives. God has glorious plans for this generation. It is time for them to know their Creator. He is calling them back to Himself for He has already prepared the way.

> *In the last days, God says,*
> *"I will pour out my Spirit upon all people.*
> *Your sons and daughters will prophesy.*
> *Your young men will see visions,*
> *and your old men will dream dreams."*
> *Acts 2:17*

CHAPTER IV
Assessments at Different Stages of Development

ASSESSMENTS DURING MIDDLE SCHOOL AND HIGH SCHOOL

As a student enters middle school (for our purposes that will be 6th grade), a student is approximately 11 or 12 years of age. We all know that the preadolescent stage can be a vulnerable time for most students. Beginning to assess "personal gifts" at this time could create the initial documentation for the student to begin to discover God's Plan and Purpose for their life. I believe this is the best time to begin assessing "personal gifts" because oftentimes middle school students lack confidence in "who they are" or "who they are becoming". The assessment process when done during middle or high school can assist a student in identifying "what makes them tick" which can be a valuable asset in a preadolescent or an adolescent. There is value in drawing out the "personal gifts" in young people. I have seen it chart a course in a young person's life toward amazing directions (all part of God's Plan and Purpose). I have also seen the opposite of that. A reckless, directionless, and unguided young person who gets involved in things that take them far from God's Plan and Purpose. Parents have the amazing opportunity to impact what direction their children go, but it is not done without prayer, intention, and hard work.

I believe when a student starts to learn about the qualities of their personality, for instance, the student starts to understand how they interact in the world around them. A positive note with this may be a student who begins to "discover" their "personal gifts" and can begin to learn how to best use them.

Of course, as the student works their way through the middle school and high school years, many changes will occur. Even through all of these changes, God has a plan and a purpose for every child. Parents can help their child discover God's Plan and Purpose by encouraging them to seek God first before anything else when creating a post-secondary plan. Parents can also contribute much insight for the child by observing and providing feedback on the child's "personal gifts". The assessment process is very insightful and comprehensive when combined with parental observations.

IV. Assessments at Different Stages of Development

Direct your children onto the right path, and when they are older, they will not leave it.

Proverbs 22:6

How this generation of young people would benefit from understanding the true meaning of this scripture. The way he should go refers to (according to his bent). Each child is gifted with "personal" and "spiritual" gifts. Each one, unique, to just that child. What parents, teachers, coaches, youth ministers should do is help the child develop their bent. A child's "bent" is their group of personal attributes that lean toward their strengths. I like what Pastor Chad Hovind, Senior Pastor of Horizon Community Church in Cincinnati, Ohio has to say about this topic:

"So we first, understand their BENT, and then we BEND" (Hovind).

Assessments during College, Technical School, or Military Enlistment

By the time a student has graduated from high school and has matriculated to a college, technical school, or the military, they should have some indication as to what "personal gifts" or "what bent" they have. Colleges have student service centers that will provide some level of "personal gifts" assessment. I am not 100% convinced that these centers are there to help the students identify "what makes them tick". Think about it, the colleges benefit from students attending classes. I have known many students who have not only moved from college to college, but also, from major to major. Student loan debt accumulates while students are still trying to find what major is best for them.

This is not to say that colleges are not helping students with "finding themselves". Remember the 20th Century, parents would say, "Go to college and you will find yourself". However, in the 20th Century, attending and graduating from college did not cost what it costs today.

Our Technical Schools are targeted with training programs specific to career-focused degrees, certificates, and diplomas. When students enroll in these types of training programs, they are usually very directed toward entering the workforce as a trained entry-level worker.

Our Military Branches provide the opportunity to take the *ASVAB® Assessment (Armed Services Vocational Aptitude Battery)*® (United States...) while still in high school or after graduation. This assessment does draw out many of the "personal gifts" in our students and will provide valuable feedback on the types of jobs and the level of skill the job requires as part of the assessment feedback. I believe the U.S. Military Branches offer amazing opportunities for our young people including educational, healthcare, travel, retirement, and job benefits. I have witnessed more young people opting in for the military in this economy than ever before. One military recruiter I work with, left the Navy, and soon realized that the Navy offered more than any job he could have acquired in this economy, so he re-enlisted.

Assessments When Entering the Workforce

When our students choose to enter the workforce upon graduation instead of automatically enrolling in college, most parents would believe this is a bad thing. I would disagree with them. With the cost of college today, if a student takes a short time period (6 months to a year), to work in a job and get some "real world" experience and participate in assessment activities, job shadowing, and informational interviewing, the student can greatly benefit from these experiences.

If a student waits until after they leave high school to begin assessing themselves, the student must be more disciplined and intentional because the student will not have the structure of high school to keep their focus. There is nothing wrong with that. God is patient. As your child pursues God's plan and purpose, your child will discern what God has gifted them to do. God will open doors that no man can shut. God will arrange divine appointments that will lead your child toward their plan and purpose. Your child's part is to seek God so they may discern God's Purpose.

Young adults entering the workforce directly after high school (without much work experience before graduating from high school) may have some challenges previous generations did not have. I am speaking about a variety of "soft skills" that may not be fully developed mostly due to many young people being very dependent on their phones and not having appropriate interpersonal skills. In my above reference to "soft skills", I am speaking about communication, problem solving, conflict resolution, time management, and professionalism.

Recently, the Allegheny Conference and the U.S. Chamber of Commerce Foundation worked with the Campos Research Strategy Organization to produce, *"Bridging the Soft Skills Gap: Employers and New Hires Agree Soft Skills are Critical, but Their Views on Preparedness are in Stark Contrast"* (Bridging the Soft Skills...). There were five primary findings from this study:

IV. Assessments at Different Stages of Development

1) "Recent college graduates and employers agree that soft skills are important for workplace success."
2) "There is a gap between how prepared recent college graduates think they are, and how prepared employers find them to be."
3) "Recent college graduates and employers differ on which soft skills are most important."
4) "Recent college graduates and employers differ greatly on which soft skills merit training."
5) "Recent college graduates and employers agree that a certificate course in soft skills training would be beneficial for college students" (Bridging the Soft Skills…).

This study concluded that recent college graduates need "soft skills" training; therefore, how much more would high school graduates entering the workforce directly after graduation require this type of training to fare well in their new environments? I believe technology has a lot to do with this generation's lack of "soft skills" development. Even though they all have phones, how often do young people use their phones as a phone? Just recently, my daughter had texted me to let me know she arrived somewhere and I did not receive the text. I waited an appropriate amount of time and still did not hear from her. I was concerned at first and then I received a text from her and she said, "My texts were not sending, now they are sending." I asked her, "Why didn't you just call me to let me know you had arrived?" After all, it is a phone!

> *For even when we were with you, this we*
> *did command you,*
> *That if any one is not willing to work,*
> *Neither let him eat.*
> 2 Thessalonians 3:10

Every generation goes through the process of assimilating into the workforce in their own way and in their own time. Because this generation is such a large group, employers are having a challenging time contending with them. Through doing the research for this book, I came across a former business teacher who has developed a business around helping corporate organizations to deal with working with millennials. His business provides training to managers who work with a declining work ethic in America (with an emphasis on the millennials) and how to motivate them to be productive in the 21st Century Workplace. About a hundred years ago when my grandfather migrated here from Dublin, Ireland, he and his counterparts did not need to be motivated to perform on the job. They wanted to keep

IV. Assessments at Different Stages of Development

a roof over their heads and food on the table. That's all they needed. By blessing our children with a better life than we had, children do not get the blessing of knowing how to work. Teaching children to know how to work is a blessing to the child for the rest of the child's life and even to the next generation.

Work gives people purpose. When a person enjoys the work they are doing, it doesn't really feel like work. When a person is doing the work meant for them, God's Purpose will manifest itself in that person's life. This person can achieve much in life.

If a student waits to assess their "personal gifts" after high school and while they are working, this time could be well spent in listening and obeying what they believe God has purposed them to do and reflecting on the assessment results.

Chapter V
What About the "Gap Year"?

Out of School Youth

According to a U.S. Bureau of Labor Statistics and a Current Population Survey (Bureau of Labor...), there are 652,000 out of school youth who never graduated from high school and 647,000 out of school youth who graduated from high school and are not working or are underemployed (Bureau of Labor...). That's well over 1 million youth who are just existing. How sad is that? God has "personal" and spiritual gifts in these youth that are going unharvested. There is such untapped potential in these young people. I believe it is the enemy of their souls stealing what God has for them.

Statistically speaking, our Out of School Youth (18 and 19 year olds who have graduated or dropped out of school) (Steinberg) can greatly benefit from taking a Gap Year. On the site www.americangap.org (The American Gap Association), Gap Year Data & Benefits page:

"Taking a structured Gap Year invariably serves to develop the individual into a more focused student with a better sense of purpose and engagement in the world" (American Gap Association).

In Joseph O'Shea's book on the Gap Year, *"Gap Year: How Delaying College Changes People in Ways the World Needs"*, he has conducted research on students who have taken "structured" gap years. He discusses the positive and negative sides of taking a gap year between high school graduation and college in his book and he discusses the changes that occur in the students from having participated in a "Gap Year" (O'Shea 2-14).

If a student purposefully uses a 6-month or 1-year time period after high school to prepare for post-secondary endeavors, the student will greatly benefit from this investment of time and contemplation. This structure requires discipline and maturity on the part of the student. A "Gap Year" can be "unstructured" too; however, if a young person has no directed activities or goals to pursue in this time before post-secondary pursuits, it can lead to negative experiences. Remember, the old saying, "An idle mind is the devil's workshop"? Structured, purposeful, directed activities to pursue God's Plan and Purpose will produce better outcomes than unstructured, aimless, and directionless activities.

V. What About the "Gap Year"?

The enemy of your child's soul wants your child to be distracted and off course. The enemy's goals are accomplished in this generation when unstructured, aimless, and directionless activities are what a young person goes after. So when these things are in place, the enemy's goals can be achieved in a young person's life. And it can happen with just a small encounter with getting off course. Parents want better for their sons and daughters. We must be deliberate in helping our children to seek God's Plan and Purpose for their lives. It takes time, intention, and perseverance, but the results will be nothing short of God's Best in a child's life. If a student has not yet sought God's Plan or Purpose for their life, this time could serve the student in intentionally seeking God's Heart. Proper assessment of various personal attributes would be valuable information for the student to attain during this structured time in between high school graduation and college admission or any other post-secondary endeavor.

"Gap Year" .....Getting More Attention

When our high school students graduate, more of them are choosing the "Gap Year" because they are "undecided" about what direction they should take. I believe this is a good choice instead of going to college, starting the student loan cycle, and starting a college major that may or may not be the right path for a person. Students who graduate high school and are unsure of what direction or college major to pursue would benefit in many ways by taking a "gap year". During this year, students have the opportunity to gain job experience, conduct career exploration, participate in assessment of personal attributes, learn about the 21st Century Labor Market, and seek direction. As discussed in Chapter 4, when students take time after graduation to assess "personal gifts" and get some direction, they will benefit. When young adults (just out of high school) take a structured "Gap Year" they can learn much about themselves to assist them in obtaining direction to create a career path to begin. The key is that the student is participating in structured activities such as:

1) Assessments (Personal and Spiritual Gifts)
2) Work (Full or Part Time)
3) Career Exploration and Researching College Options (Job Shadows & College Visits)
4) Skill Development (Improving Academic Skills, Soft Skills, Computer Skills)
5) Personal Finance (Establishing a Checking Account, Money Management)
6) Networking (Establishing Personal and Professional Contacts)

V. What About the "Gap Year"?

WHAT IS CAREER MATURITY?

Dr. Kenneth Gray speaks about "career maturity" in both *Other Ways to Win: Creating Alternatives for High School Graduates* and *Getting Real: Helping Teens Find Their Future.* Dr. Kenneth Gray breaks down what career maturity involves:

1) They understand that career direction, even a tentative one, is as important to postsecondary success as good grades.
2) They have made tentative choices by the 10th grade.
3) They have taken actions that would verify these choices during their final two years of high school.
4) They use these decisions as one focus for postsecondary planning (Gray 8).

When I read the above-mentioned list, I thought that is exactly what our students should have while in high school. Unfortunately, for a multitude of reasons, that is not what most students experience in 10th grade. Students are consumed with academic pursuits, extracurricular activities, sports, community service, part-time jobs, and social engagements. Of course, all of these are vital. When would they even have time to achieve "career maturity" when so few of the things they are involved in while in high school have anything to do with the elements of becoming "career mature"? I agree with Dr. Gray that 10th graders should have a tentative plan toward a career path. This generation of students is using 20th Century Thinking about going off to college to find themselves and do not realize that the cost of college tuition has increased over 250% and has continued to increase since the 1980s. Many high school students jump into the academic honors program as they enter high school, which is commendable, but don't have any idea why they eventually take Honors Geometry or Honors Chemistry. What if the student dislikes both of these classes, but they have the ability to perform well in the classes? Would the student be better served if, even before they entered high school, they knew that the courses they enrolled in while in high school would draw out strengths, interests, personality attributes, and values? I believe not only would it benefit the student to know if the courses they are taking in high school would draw out their strengths, interests, personality attributes, and values, but also the student would be motivated to succeed in those courses.

I also believe that exposure to the "World of Work" would move students along in their pursuit of career maturity because they would have opportunities to learn about careers and what they would like to pursue, or even not to pursue in the "World of Work." Knowing what you don't want to pursue is as valuable as knowing what you do you want to pursue. We all know someone who went to college for a degree, transitioned into the workforce, and subsequently hated the career they spent money and time pursuing. Exposure to the reality of that career prior to college could have saved those two very important resources.

> *For we are God's masterpiece. He has created us anew in Christ Jesus, so we can do the good things he planned for us long ago.*
>
> *Ephesians 2:10*

Possible Outcomes of Taking the "Gap Year"

Pursuing God's Plan and Purpose intentionally and contemplatively during a structured "Gap Year" can produce amazing results, especially if during the "Gap Year" a young person seeks first what God has purposed them to do. This time can provide opportunities for the young adults that they would never have while still in high school without the pressures of maintaining grades, preparing for standardized testing, and balancing all of the priorities of high school. Some students use their "Gap Year" to travel abroad, to learn about new cultures/languages, to serve in community service projects, to do missions work, and the list goes on. If the "Gap Year" is taken seriously and pursued with intention, I believe it can be life changing for a student. According to Joseph O'Shea in his book, *"Gap Year: How Delaying College Changes People in Ways the World Needs,"* students who participated in a "Gap Year" for self-exploration saw changes in the following areas:

1) Understanding Themselves
2) Being New
3) Independence
4) Control
5) Resilience and Emotional Regulation
6) Making a Difference
7) Self Confidence
8) "Grown Up" (O'Shea 24, 26…)

From my perspective of working and observing young people in this generation, the above-mentioned experiences from a structured "Gap Year" sound like

V. What About the "Gap Year"?

they are worthwhile. Therefore, for some students in this generation, the structured "Gap Year" is a good option for young people to come to an understanding of who they are and what their purpose in life will be.

CHAPTER VI
Hindrances to Finding God's Plan and Purpose

*I warned you when you were prosperous,
but you replied, 'Don't bother me.'
You have been that way since childhood—
you simply will not obey me!*
                                   Jeremiah 22:21

DISOBEDIENCE

Our disobedience causes many problems. Disobedience can hinder a person's life in many ways. Initially, when we do not receive Christ, we demonstrate disobedience to what God has already done for us. God created us with free will and we should choose to be obedient to God's Will, not our own will. Being obedient to God is a daily choice. Being obedient to God's Will for our lives must be intentional and done with purpose.

> *Don't be fooled by those who try to excuse these sins, for the anger of God will fall on all who disobey him.*
>
> *Ephesians 5:6*

Just reading that scripture is a reminder to me that obedience is a choice that we should make every day to spare the wrath of God upon our lives. Obedience has its' blessings and disobedience has its' curses. In the Book of Deuteronomy in the 28th Chapter, the Blessings of Obedience and the Curses of Disobedience are covered. In His Book, *The Hiram Code: Discovering the Ancient Secrets for Favor in the Last Days,* Dr. Ron Phillips discusses Psalm 105:37-45. This scripture discusses how the Israelite People were blessed because they obeyed God. Dr. Phillips' interpretation of this scripture was listed in his book:

1) They enjoyed prosperity. (Psalm 105:37)
2) There was none sick. (Psalm 105:37)
3) God gave them victory over the enemy. (Psalm 105:38)
4) All their needs were met. (Psalm 105:40-41)
5) Joy and gladness filled the camp. (Psalm 105:43)
6) He gave them their inheritance. (Psalm 105:44) (Phillips 19).

VI. Hindrances to Finding God's Plan and Purpose

Wow, being obedient to what God says does all of that! Why would we choose disobedience if we know what obedience rewards us with? **Again, obedience has its' blessings and disobedience has its' curses.** This generation needs to know these truths. What potential this generation has if they are obedient to God's Word! What loss of potential this generation has if they are disobedient to God's Word!

LACK OF SELF REFLECTION AND DISCERNMENT

Too many young people do not take the time to self reflect before going off to college. Taking time to reflect and discern God's Will is a process through time and study in the Word of God. It can be done through a deliberate effort on our parts. I have heard students reporting such things as the following statements after participating in assessments and job shadow experiences:

1) It gave me confidence and I was more confident of what I wanted to do.
2) I felt more aware of myself and my personality traits.
3) I am excited about my future now.
4) It helped me understand how important it is to know yourself before selecting a college major.

5) These experiences helped me to know what to focus on and what to eliminate as I move forward toward my future.
6) I decreased my anxiety about life after high school; I was afraid of making a wrong choice.
7) I am glad I went on that job shadow; I eliminated that career.

This process of observing middle and high school students learning about their "personal gifts" has been so interesting to witness. When I work with students in doing this work, I usually begin to tell them, "You are going to work on your favorite subject today — YOU!" They are interested and engaged immediately. I feel privileged to be able to work with students as they learn about themselves and the untapped potential in each of them. When they finish, I let them know that this is valuable information for planning their future. I meet with the students in class and discuss their individual results and then we start generating ideas for pursuing career paths that reflect assessment results. I am sure to present all of the post-secondary options available to them, not just a 4-year college option. I want them to know all the options to reach their goals and help them develop a strategy to reduce the costs of reaching their goals. Many of them have anxiety and fear of making the wrong decisions when they graduate and

VI. Hindrances to Finding God's Plan and Purpose

sometimes this hinders the development of a "plan" as they are transitioning out of high school. Other variables that may hinder the development of a "tentative post-secondary plan" are lack of confidence, lack of exposure to careers, lack of role models, lack of motivation, and lack of emotional or career maturity. Maybe a little of all of those things are going on with a student. In his book, *Getting Real: Helping Teens Find their Future*, Dr. Kenneth Gray points out three behaviors of "career mature" teens.

"Attitudes
    *Appreciation for the importance of planning;
    *Willingness to face reality;

Skills
    *Career Exploration Skills;
    *Decision-Making Skills;

Knowledge of Self
    *Understanding of self in relation to the world of work;
    *Understanding abilities, aptitudes, and self-relation to the world of work" (Gray 109).

With relation to Dr. Gray's "Career Mature Behaviors of Adolescents" (Gray 109), I could not agree more. However, as I reflected on those behaviors with relation to today's average teen, I realized that many of those behaviors are not demonstrated by them. Therefore, many teens are not "career mature" when they matriculate to their post-secondary experiences and what they do not realize is that lacking career maturity will hinder their success. All of those behaviors should be developed and enhanced in middle and high school if the students are provided opportunities to develop the qualities of being "career mature", but it will not be by accident or a coincidence.

Matriculating to college immediately after high school is the expectation that has been put on many students by their parents, high schools, friends, and society as a whole. The issue here is that not all students who get accepted and enroll in college actually will benefit and graduate from college. Some of them are not ready academically, socially, or emotionally mature enough to accept the responsibilities of "going off to college". That is reflective in the high college drop-out rate. Because there is such a huge difference between what high school is like vs. what college is like, many of these students are not transitioning well. College is not for everyone and that should be acceptable in our society.

The website www.chronicleforhighereducation.com (The Chronicle of...) keeps track of the college completion rates per state, private vs. public, 4 year school vs. 2 year school. I recently viewed the site for the Commonwealth

VI. Hindrances to Finding God's Plan and Purpose

of Pennsylvania for the 4-year public university system. It reflected the following for Number of graduates:

41.6% four years (almost 42 students graduate in four years, what happened to the other 59 students?)

62.9% six years (almost 63 students graduate in six years, what happened to the other 38 students?) (The Chronicle of...)

I am not writing this to discredit the public university system in PA. The system is a good one. I am writing this to draw attention to the fact that not all students who enroll in college actually graduate from college. These are the statistics that no one ever hears about, but are the reality today.

Worldly Interventions — Drugs, Alcohol, Bad Influences

This generation is under attack by the enemy of their souls. So many undirected, unguided youth are involved in illegal drugs, alcohol, and other bad influences (gangs, drugs/alcohol usage, crime, pornography, depression, suicidal thoughts). Because many of our young people do not know where these "worldly interventions" are coming from, they cannot fend off this enemy. The enemy has a plan of destruction for their lives, but God has a plan of abundant life for them. The enemy's best tool is deception so if he can deceive a young person to believe that getting involved in using drugs and alcohol is a "cool thing" to do, that is the opening he needs to destroy that young person's life. If he can convince a young person to try drugs, the ultimate goal is addiction. The enemy of our souls only needs a crack in the door to enable him to kick the door wide open to his plan to steal, kill, and destroy a person. We all have stories about how drug and alcohol addictions have affected someone we know or someone we love. The enemy is busy; we have to get busy revealing the enemy's plan against this generation and God's Great Plan for this generation.

Poor Decisions

When we are young, at times, we don't realize that the decisions we are making will affect and impact the remaining years of our lives. It is critical to get our youth to understand how important it is to make good decisions. So many youth seem to "throw" away this time and put off making decisions toward seeking God's Plan and Purpose for their lives. When a student makes a quick, rash decision because they feel pressured by family or friends to "do something" after high school, it will almost be like they are setting themselves up to fail. If only they could get ahold of what is inside of them (their gift sets) and be excited about pursuing God's Plan and Purpose for their lives?

> *Just as the rich rule the poor,*
> *so the borrower is servant to the lender.*
> *Proverbs 22:7*

GETTING INTO DEBT

The cost of college has gone up dramatically since the 1980s. The economics of college admissions is driven by the high demand for college entrance. When something is in demand, the cost goes up. When something is not in demand, the cost goes down. That is simple economics.

As a teacher, I highly recommend the pursuit and completion of a college degree. However, I believe because of the cost of attending college in the 21st Century, students need to develop a strategy to pursue and complete a degree with an awareness of what the debt load will be 6 months after graduation and how it will impact their adulthood. Before taking on student loan debt, students should be educated on personal finance issues such as credit, interest, and debt to income ratio. I believe that a class in personal finance should be required as a high school course for graduation. Students are subject to the financial aid industry and most of them do not fully understand all of the responsibility they are taking on when they accept the loans.

In preparation for their exit, I teach a class, "21st Century Skills" for juniors and seniors to educate them about in-demand careers, soft skills, career and technical fields, college transition, workplace readiness, and the cost of college and post-secondary education. Teaching this class has been an eye-opening experience for me. This class is an elective and I have worked with gifted, typical, and special needs students in this class. It makes sense that students of all ability levels have selected this class because all of them have a desire to transition successfully into a college, technical school, military branch, or a workplace after high school. One of the counselors from the career technical school where we send our students found out about the class and asked, "Why isn't this class mandatory for every student to graduate?" I wish I could reach every student with this information before they graduate. They all need this information; it is to the benefit of the student to receive this information before graduation.

Student Loan Debt is an enormous problem that is already having an impact on this generation. Many of them are not paying on their student loans as evidenced

VI. Hindrances to Finding God's Plan and Purpose

by the default rate. The problem with defaulting on student loans is that it is going to affect these students when they apply for a job, a mortgage, or a car loan. There is no filing bankruptcy on student loan debt. Part of the problem of students getting into debt is that they do not understand personal finance. It is easy to understand that when they go to sign their student loan disbursements at the financial aid office, they really do not fully comprehend what financial responsibility they are taking on when they sign that contract. I am in the "camp" that all high school students should be required to take a personal finance class as a high school graduation requirement. Isn't there a chance if they understood what they were signing, they would make different post-secondary decisions? At this writing, the student loan debt burden is over $1 trillion. So many young people are in tremendous debt even before they can get their adult lives started. This isn't right. The enemy of their souls seeks to have them in debt, but the One who died for them wants them to be debt-free. Jesus causes us to be prosperous, the enemy causes poverty.

When I teach a lesson on Personal Finance in my "Exploring Career Paths" class, I review such items as Gross vs. Net Income, Fixed vs. Variable Expenses, Budget, Calculating a Payment (Principle x Rate x Time in Excel), Debt to Income Ratio, Interest, Credit, and Investing.

As part of this lesson, the students are introduced to a budget template in Excel. I show them how to calculate gross and net income with a specific salary and within a specific tax bracket. In the budget template, they learn how to calculate a mortgage payment, a car payment, a student loan payment, utilities, living expenses, food, savings, and various other day-to-day expenses. It is always such an eye-opening experience for them to take time to learn how to do all of these calculations after they decide on a career, a house, and a car. They also learn how to calculate the item percentage of their whole budget so they can see how it all adds up to 100%. It takes about a week or so to teach them how to do the calculations and show them how to look up the prices of all of their budget items. At the end of the lesson, they all have a completed budget and have a "reality check" on how expensive their lives will become. This lesson has taught me that all high school students could gain a lot from this experience. They need to know about money management. Why is this not part of the core curriculum in high school? I think most parents would agree that a semester in high school to learn personal finance as a requirement of graduation is a good idea.

Chapter VII
Developing a Career Path to begin a Journey

Career Planning and When to Start

The development of a career path can be crafted at any time in a person's life. People are changing careers now more than ever. With the proliferation of technology changing as quickly as it does, it is possible to upgrade your educational level and/or technical skills from the comfort of your home on your own schedule. However, is it possible to start developing a career path as early as middle school? If students are involved in assessments that help them discover their "personal gifts" as young as 6th grade (let's say 12 years old) and the students are also involved in career exploration activities and experiences, I would say those students could begin charting a course toward a career path. If students have the opportunity to learn their "spiritual gifts" as well as their "personal gifts", that is a bonus for them. These insights are invaluable when a student learns about these gifts during middle or high school.

In his book, *"Getting Real: Helping Teens Find Their Future"*, Dr. Kenneth Gray discusses the importance of career planning for teens:

> **"Graduating from high school with verified yet tentative career interests leads to both post-secondary success and a stable career pattern later in life. Teens have two choices: They can let fate and labor market Darwinism decide their future or they can be proactive and plan for success" (Gray 70).**

Obviously, the better option is to be proactive and plan for success. However, how many of our young people do not invest time into being proactive and planning for success through developing a career plan?

I recently read an article by Dr. Genevra Walters, *"A Forward-Thinking Superintendent Details How She Transformed her General Education Program into a Series of Career Academies"* (Walters). This article highlights the work that Dr. Walters has done in transforming middle school and high school programs in the Kankakee Schools in Illinois into career academies. The students of this district are involved in Interest Inventories that direct instruction toward a career academy within the district. The tracks offered in this District are Freshmen Academy, Business Academy, Medical Academy and STEM. One of the benefits the district has seen since implementing their STEM program is "an increase in student performance in reading and math" (Walters). One could conclude, with the career academies in place in this district, students are more focused and directed toward subjects that interest them.

Two years ago, my principal asked me to write a curriculum for a class on developing a career path. He knew I would be interested in this type of course. I identified a textbook that I wanted to use after conducting research with a few publishing companies. I chose *"Investigating Your Career"* by Tena Crews and Ann Jordan. The class was named, "Exploring Career Paths," and at the writing of this book, I have taught the class twice. I have to say it has been very interesting to observe the reactions and conversations of the students in these classes. The National Career Clusters (Career Clusters...) are presented in this textbook. The students participate in assessments to identify their "P * A * T * H" (Jordan and Crews 109) Tena Crews and Ann Jordan illustrate what

P * A * T * H (Jordan and Crews 109) stands for in their book (Jordan and Crews 109):

P (assions) → (Interests)

A (ttitude) → (Personality)

T (alents) → (Strengths)

H (heart)© → (Values)

} Jordan, Ann K. and Crews, Tena B.

Investigating Your Career, South-Western

Cengage Learning, Mason, OH, 2013, Page 109

After the students complete assessments to find these personal attributes, they gather the information onto a Career Cluster Table and begin to conduct research on careers that match the data they collected. They are required to have a Plan A and a Plan B (two career clusters) that match their results. This is not to say that the student has to immediately pursue a degree in Plan A or Plan B; it is to say the student now has an idea of what personal attributes could possibly be aligned with possible careers. The data the students receive about themselves is eye-opening and insightful. They research possible careers in the career clusters that are associated with the data that is gathered from their assessments.

Tools to Use: Informational Interviews, Job Shadows, Mentoring

When students seek and experience opportunities to participate in an informational interview or go on a job shadow, they learn about the realities of a career. They would never be able to learn about these realities in a classroom or from a textbook. These experiences allow students to get first-hand knowledge about a career, experience a work day, and get the students exposed to the realities of what it takes to achieve the career of the person they are shadowing or interviewing.

It has been so interesting to see how students have embraced the opportunity to learn about a career by participating in a job shadow experience. One of my observations is that as I worked with all four grade levels in high school some of the older students were not "ready" to participate in job shadow experiences while some of the younger counterparts were excited to participate. I wonder if being close to their graduation without a tentative plan caused hesitation in participating in a job shadow while the younger students were eager to participate because they knew they had time to "find their way"? I had a student participate in a job shadow toward the end of her freshmen year, that she arranged herself, in an operating room. When she returned to school, she was motivated to plan a career path as either a nurse or physician. She came back so motivated to pursue the best academic program through her remaining years in high school. I was proud of her! This experience has now motivated this young lady to realize how important her academic record is in correlation to her future career. She came back to school, wrote a two-page report on her experience, and was ready to do her best in school. That is a win-win for both the student and the school.

I recommend starting this process in either 10th or 11th grade to allow the students enough time to "learn about what makes them tick" and to begin an experiential career exploration process through participating in informational interviews and spending time on job shadows. When a student is "career mature" and "emotionally mature", they will benefit the most from connecting the idea of a career with the reality of what it is really like by networking with a professional in the field.

Recently, I assigned a 500-word essay to the students in the Exploring Career Paths Class. After the students had learned about career clusters and had participated in some assessment work, they were asked to identify two interesting career clusters and write the essay on how their "personal gifts" were associated with those

VII. Developing a Career Path to begin a Journey

career clusters. One of the essays that was turned in was from a senior who I had worked with since his junior year on assessments, informational interviews, and job shadow experiences. In his essay, he wrote about how his generation has amazing opportunities to create the lives they want because of the assessment tools that are available today and how they can learn about a career before going to college through the above-mentioned experiences. I really enjoyed reading his essay because this was a young man who was focused, motivated, and excited about his future. I believe all high school students should leave our schools like this. It is possible for our students to do this work before leaving our high schools, but it has to be intentional and purposeful. It will not happen by accident.

Mentoring is an underutilized tool we should be tapping into to develop this next generation. So many young people would greatly benefit from a caring, responsible adult who has a career of interest to a young person. It takes time and energy to mentor, but the results can be phenomenal. When caring adults pour time and energy into a young person, the impact can be immeasurable.

Interview Colleges, Instead of Them Interviewing You

Once a student achieves a good academic record in high school, the letter and e-mail campaign begins from the colleges and universities. With so many options available for students, there is much competition for them to enroll and attend the colleges that are recruiting them. Recently, I had been invited to bring students even as young as the 8th grade to a 4-year college recruitment event. The admission representatives are developing strategies for reaching students even before they get into high school by having the students speak with college faculty and take tours of college campuses. Most people may think that is "too early" to start this process, but what if a student has this experience of going to a college to learn about the admission requirements before they even start high school and this experience allows the student to realize how important it is to make the most of the 720 days they will have in high school? This experience could be a "game changer" for the student. Some students like the idea of just taking the courses related to obtaining a two-year degree without the liberal arts curriculum. Obviously, it is the choice of the student whether they want to pursue a 4-year degree. Students need to realize that because there is so much competition for them to enroll in a post-secondary institution, students are the ones who are "in-demand". Of course, the colleges, universities, technical schools, military branches are not going to let the students know this. This generation has so much opportunity, but many of them are filled with anxiety and fear about what the future holds for them, and they do not have any idea of how recruiters are competing to recruit them. Technical schools are getting more active in the recruitment of high school students as well. Recently, I received an e-mail from a technical school that I work with that contained a video. The video promoted a "Signing Day" as a recruitment tool for their programs. Technical school recruiters are connecting with high school students while they are attending a career and technology center to recruit them for their Associate Degree Programs. These students already have a foundation in their choice of a vocational field and that will assist them in pursuing and completing their Associate Degree.

College, University, Technical, and Military Recruiters are using many new strategies to find and attract new students/recruits. Some of these strategies include:

1) Going to the student's home to visit with the prospective student and parents
2) Meeting with students during school

3) Participating in College/Career Fairs in the High Schools
4) E-mailing the student and their parents
5) Calling the student on their home and cell phones
6) College for a Weekend Programs
7) Meeting with prospective students in a local eatery to connect with the student individually
8) Creating customized webpages to enable students to learn about the college
9) Junk mail campaigns to recruit the students
10) Identifying students as early as 8th grade to recruit for their colleges

I am sure there are more strategies being developed to recruit the students of this generation for post-secondary endeavors. As I recall, in the 20th Century, recruiters did not have to try so hard to recruit students. This generation is in demand because of the retiring baby boomers leaving the workforce and the ever expanding career and technical needs of the 21st Century.

When a student is going through the process of selecting colleges to apply, they should definitely spend time on the campus and get to know what it is like to be a student there. Not only should the student "interview" admission staff, the student should meet with current students and get an impression of what a "day in the life" of a student is actually like. Of course, the colleges the student selects should be colleges that the student is confident they will be accepted to or have already been accepted. Yes, this is an investment of time and energy, but with the cost of college today, a student should be "doing their homework" before beginning such a huge investment of money and time.

CAREER CENTERS ON COLLEGE CAMPUSES

Not only should a "potential" student interview the admission staff at a college or university they are interested in attending, the student should inquire about the services of the college's career center. Of course, the pursuit of a college degree is an honorable one and should enable the student to expand their horizons, develop and enhance critical thinking skills, and receive a quality holistic education. In addition to all of those expectations, the completion of a college degree in the 21st century should enable the student to begin in a career, pay student loan debt, and start pursuing the "American Dream". So to ensure that a student will be able to do all of those things, the student should "interview" the staff within the Career Center of a college they may be interested in attending. The student should know the job placement rankings for the colleges they are applying. Most students are not thinking about career placement issues when they are in the "college search" process. However, since the 21st Century Economy is competitive in nature, these students should consider thinking about the career placement services of the colleges they are considering.

SUCCESS IN COLLEGE.....WHAT IT TAKES TO GET THE DEGREE

The difference between what it takes to succeed and graduate from a high school could not be further from what it takes to succeed and graduate from college today. Much has changed in the 21st Century. There are many changes to the way high school teachers have to teach and those changes have affected how students learn. In my opinion, the mandatory, standardized testing requirements have created a loss of "the love of learning". When these same students matriculate to college, they are expecting to have to memorize facts and complete a certain amount of questions within the time period given. To succeed in college, you have to be able to critically think, analyze information, compare and contrast ideas, problem solve, and create solutions. Our high school students need more of these experiences before they transition into college if they are to succeed and graduate from a college or university.

VII. Developing a Career Path to begin a Journey

Many high school students are matriculating to a college campus upon graduation whether they have any guidance, direction, or academic ability to succeed when they get there. It is just "the expected" thing to do. Students have not necessarily learned the "soft skills" to succeed on a college campus and this may be one of the factors contributing to the high college dropout rate. I have spoken to several college admission representatives who have reported that they have seen students drop out, not just because of academic problems, but because of a lack of "soft skills" and independent living skills.

Students need to be emotionally, mentally, academically, and physically prepared to handle the responsibilities of college life. Not all the students we are sending off to university are ready to succeed when they get there. I believe when students enter 9th grade or even in late middle school, they can start engaging in activities to be able to handle the responsibilities of college life. Parents are the coaches to help their children become emotionally, mentally, and academically prepared to handle the responsibilities of college life. This happens only through a very intentional process.

To succeed in a university, our students have to be able to manage priorities, time, deadlines, independent living (if on campus), and the whole academic experience. A successful transition from high school to a college campus requires academic, emotional, and career maturity. Students must understand that professors will indeed hold them accountable as an adult for the requirements of the class. Their grades in college will be reflective of a variety of assignments, papers, presentations, mid-term exams, and final exams. Time management is a critical skill for a student to succeed in college. This may be a skill many entering college freshmen need to work on for a successful transition to college life.

Many colleges offer a "freshmen seminar" course now to help smooth the transition for these students when they get onto a college campus. Prior to that, some universities may offer summer programs to connect with potential incoming students in an effort to recruit them early.

Chapter VIII
What Paths to Pursue Your Purpose?

I am a junior in high school and just starting to explore all of my choices! I will invest time and energy during my junior and senior years to learn about what God has for me.

- College/University
- Military Enlistment
- Career/Technical Training (in High School or College)
- Apprenticeship Training
- School to Work

What is God's Plan to Fulfill God's Purpose for Your Child?

Career/Technical Education While in High School

Depending on the K-12 system the student is attending, the career/technical education options usually start between 9th and 10th grade. By the time a student starts high school, a student and their parents will have an idea of whether the student is "academic/college bound" or "career-technical bound". The student's transcript will illustrate strengths and weaknesses to assist the student and the parents in identifying what educational direction would best serve the student. Based on the academic experience of the student, the parents and the student should be able to discern if obtaining a college degree or obtaining career technical training would best serve the student. If the student is more inclined toward "career-technical" fields, I highly recommend that the student seriously consider participating in the training offered while the student is still in high school. When looking at the Labor Statistics between 2017 to 2024, there are many career technical fields that are in demand and only require an Associate's Degree as opposed to a Bachelor's Degree. Since the American Workforce will need more career and technically trained workers, it is time to let our American High School Students in on this information.

VIII. What Paths to Pursue Your Purpose

It has been somewhat "taboo" to suggest to a high school parent that a student should consider the career-technical education program while in high school. The benefit of enrolling in career technical training in high school enables the student to obtain a marketable skill while still being able to have the option to pursue a college degree beyond high school. Just because someone chose the career technical program in high school does not mean that the student automatically will not go to college. What it does mean is that the student will have a marketable skill while earning a college degree. That is a good thing!

Another benefit of having a student attend a career technical training program while in high school is the opportunity to earn an industry-standard certification, such as taking a NOCTI® (National Occupational Competency Testing Institute)® (NOCTI) Exam. NOCTI® (NOCTI) offers exams in the following career clusters:

"Agriculture, Food & Natural Resources"
"Architecture & Construction"
"Arts, A/V Technology & Communication"
"Business, Management & Administration"
"Education & Training"
"Finance"
"Health Science"
"Hospitality & Tourism"

"Human Services"
"Information Technology"
"Law, Public Safety, and Security" (Career Clusters...)

The NOCTI® (NOCTI) testing opportunities will not be available in every Career Technical Center. The testing is based on the career technical programs that are being offered within the center. I have worked with students who have taken these exams. When a student passes a NOCTI® (NOCTI) exam, it builds their confidence and prepares them for the field of work with a credential that holds weight with an employer. Another opportunity for students to engage in is skill development through their participation in SkillsUSA® (SkillsUSA) competitions throughout the school year. SkillsUSA® (SkillsUSA) holds state and national competitions in fields such as automotive manufacturing technology, carpentry, computer programming, cosmetology, culinary arts, masonry, web design, welding, and many more (SkillsUSA). The skills students are acquiring through the training and participation in competitions will transfer easily to a "real-world" job opportunity whether the student goes directly to work or transitions into a post-secondary opportunity. Cooperative education opportunities that connect trained students to entry-level job openings while still in high school is another potential outcome of career technical education. I had a student a

VIII. What Paths to Pursue Your Purpose

few years ago in a "Career Education" class in 9th grade and he sought my advice for entering a career technical program for 10th through 12th grades. He decided to take the electrical trades training program. I supported and encouraged him with this decision to enter the electrical trades career technical program because he was so interested in it and he loved working with his hands. In his senior year, he was able to get placed with an electrical contractor through a cooperative education opportunity. He remained working for the electrical contractor after graduation and subsequently was hired by an Oil and Gas Business and doubled his salary. I remember he came back to see me at school and was thrilled with the opportunity he had and wanted to thank me for helping him when he was making this decision. I was so happy for him and I was very proud of him as well.

The option of cooperation education ("working part of the day while still in high school") is a viable one. That is why I think that offering a cooperative education experience in every high school, not just at the career technical centers, would benefit all students. If they were on a job during part of their day in the last semester of high school or even the entire senior year, they would gain much: Earn money, gain "real-world" job experience, develop emotional and career maturity, and expose themselves to potential careers, and lastly, pay taxes.

College or University

As mentioned earlier, once a student establishes a solid academic record in high school by taking and completing rigorous coursework in 9th and 10th grade, the student begins receiving literature from prospective colleges and universities in the mail and on e-mail. There is much competition for the admissions counselors to recruit the best and brightest students for their freshmen classes in the upcoming year and the years to come. In the opportunities I have in working with college and technical school recruiters, I am hearing them all say the same thing about competing for students. These students are in demand, but most of them do not understand competition so they can use it to their advantage when seeking acceptance and scholarship opportunities. If an academically-sound student understood the competitive nature of the college admissions process, they could use the opportunities offered by one college to have another college compete for them.

College and University recruiters will request the opportunity to present their schools usually once a year in my "21st Century Skills" and "Exploring Career Paths" classes. These presentations are informative and usually

VIII. What Paths to Pursue Your Purpose

offer a "real world" lesson as part of the presentations. Because I believe it is important to provide these "real-world" opportunities to high school students, I welcome them a few times a month during a semester. It also gives the students an opportunity to engage and interact with a new face. Some students in the generation are hesitant to reach out and connect with a new person "face to face." Technology is a wonderful tool for this generation, but nothing will replace the experience of "face to face" human interaction.

College and University Admissions Representatives are very supportive of high school teachers bringing students to spend a day on their campuses. I have opportunities every year to visit colleges and technical schools on field trips. We are always welcomed with an admissions presentation, a campus tour, and usually lunch for all the students in a campus cafeteria. These are great opportunities for students to spend a day on a college campus, ask questions about majors, scholarships, life on campus, and become familiar with the atmosphere of the college. After these visits, I encourage the students to follow up with another visit with their parents and have a list of questions for the second visit specific to the student's college/career path. With the way things are today, both parents and students need to feel comfortable with the college's environment before the student arrives on campus.

One of the concerns I have is the high college dropout rate. I have read many websites that catalog statistics on college completion rates. From these various sites, I have learned that the United States has the highest college dropout rate in the industrialized world. I believe there are many variables and factors that have created this situation. Many of the students who have dawned the college classroom should have chosen another post-secondary option. Many of them lack time management skills, lack self-knowledge (identifying a major or career path to pursue), lack academic preparation for the rigor of the college workload, lack emotional maturity and career maturity, and lack financial resources to continue pursuing their degrees. These are just a few reasons why many of our young people do not complete their degrees.

According to Horn & Berger (2005), 66% of high school graduates pursue college enrollment upon graduating from high school (Horn and Berger). This number has changed some, but college enrollment has remained over 60% upon high school graduation. Going off to college is the expected behavior that is why the statistics are high. As I was conducting research for writing this book, I found much data on the demand for Associate Degrees or Technical Degrees going forward in the 21st Century. However, we have millions of young people on college and university campuses pursuing bachelor and master's

VIII. What Paths to Pursue Your Purpose

degrees who don't have this information. Additionally, these students are accumulating millions of dollars in student loan debt. That's not to say their pursuit of a bachelor's degree is not worthy, but shouldn't they know the realities of the labor market? In "Pathways to Prosperity: Meeting the Challenge of Preparing Young Americans for the 21st Century" by Harvard's Graduate School of Education when referring to a study by the Center for Education and Workforce at Georgetown University (Symonds, et al).

> "The Georgetown Center projects that 14 million job openings—nearly half of those that will be filled by workers with post-secondary education—will go to people with an associate's degree or occupational certificate. Many of these will be in "middle-skill" occupations such as electrician, and construction manager, dental hygienist, paralegal and police officer. While these jobs may not be as prestigious as those filled by B.A. holders, they pay a significant premium over many jobs open to those with just a high school degree. More surprisingly, they pay more than many of the jobs held by those with a bachelor's degree. In fact, 27 percent of people with

post-secondary licenses or certificates—credentials short of an associate's degree—earn more than the average bachelor's degree recipient" (Symonds, et al).

As I continue to learn more about the labor market needs of the 21st Century, the more convinced I am that the differential for success does not depend on just having a college degree. The differential for success is in having the college degree with technical abilities. It is time for all high school and college students to have a solid academic background, strong technical skills, and a solid work ethic for when they enter the workforce.

Technical College

These colleges are gaining momentum in the 21st Century. I have spoken with many students in this generation who do not want to pursue the 4-year degree because they do not want to take the "liberal arts" courses required. They can identify specialized training they are interested in and only want to take those courses. For these students, it is a great option. They will complete their training in 2 years or less and begin a career. One concern may be that some of these colleges are "for profit" and the tuition is high. I would caution students

VIII. What Paths to Pursue Your Purpose

to be aware of the differences among public, private, for-profit and not-for-profit schools. Most of our high school students don't know the difference between and among these options. The Technical Schools are very good at targeting high school students who are interested in their programs. As I mentioned earlier, I arrange for speakers to come into my "21st Century Skills" and "Exploring Career Paths" Classes from post-secondary schools to provide insight for the students while they are working on developing their college/career plan. I have to say that the technical school recruiters are very intentional in following up and scheduling appointments to present their programs to these potential students. When they come, they collect student data, if the students are willing to give it.

Because career and technical fields are growing so rapidly, students who attend and graduate from these types of schools are often recruited for work even before they have completed their program of study. I knew of a career technical school that was starting a welding program in the fall semester a few years ago. Welders must have been in demand in our area. The school received a call early in the year from an owner of a welding business and the owner wanted to hire 50 welders. The school had not started the training, but the workers were already in demand.

MILITARY BRANCH

What great opportunities our military branches offer this generation of students! After a student takes the *ASVAB® (Armed Services Vocational Aptitude Battery) (United States...)*, they will receive a follow-up meeting with the military recruiter to discuss their options for a job assignment in the military branch they may be seeking to join. When a student understands the data from their *ASVAB®* (United States...) scores, the student will be made aware of what military positions they might be suited for based on their performance on the test. This may be the first time a student understands how they perform on a test and how that correlates to an entry-level military assignment within the military branch they are interested in joining. The *ASVAB®* (United States...) will report the following types of data to the student:

1) Your Interests: Holland's Theory of Career Choice: Realistic, Conventional, Enterprising, Social, Artistic, Investigative® (Holland Codes...)

2) Skills and Abilities in Career Exploration Areas such as Verbal, Math,
Science, and Technical Skills
ASVAB® (United States...) Test Areas:
General Science

Arithmetic Reasoning
Word Knowledge
Paragraph Comprehension
Mathematics Knowledge
Electronics Information
Auto and Shop Information
Mechanical Comprehension

3) Work Values (United States...)
I receive phone calls and e-mails from military recruiters every year to schedule presentations in my classes. The recruiters also participate in the college/career fair we hold every year. The presentations reveal what the recruiters are seeking in recruits, the pay grades, the travel benefits, the family benefits, and the educational benefits. Whether or not a student has a college/career path developed by their senior year or not, it is worth the time to learn about the numerous advantages military enlistment offers in the 21st Century.

ONLINE DEGREES

As I write this book, we are 17 years into the 21st century. We all have to admit, technology has affected everything we do and how we do it. We now have an opportunity to take a class at any time, whether live or archived, from anywhere we are as well as show up on a Monday, Wednesday, and Friday from 9:00 to 9:50 for College English 101. Getting a degree online is becoming more credible and popular as we are approaching the end of the second decade of the 21st century. The flexibility that an online degree offers appeals to many people in diverse situations: Working adults seeking their first degree, Stay-at-Home Moms who want to re-enter the workforce, Military Personnel, Career Changers, and Professionals seeking advanced degrees.

I remember getting another certification area added onto my teaching certificate by completing 12 credits online with a state university which enabled me to take the certification exam. I really enjoyed the classes from the comfort of my home and being able to do the coursework at my own pace. With tools such as Skype® and Zoom®, college professors can plan a course where students can sign in and participate from wherever they are. Recently, I attended an online class with the University of Iowa to gain a certification as a "Biz Innovator" Instructor from the Jacobson Institute of Youth Entrepreneurship. The class only had 10 teachers in it who were from California to Maine in location. It was interesting to learn about what other business teachers were doing in their schools.

Online training programs in technology fields are also emerging. The two that come to mind are

VIII. What Paths to Pursue Your Purpose

www.udacity.com (Udacity) and https://skillcrush.com (Skillcrush). Udacity© was started by a former Google Fellow and Stanford Research Professor, Sebastian Thrun, and Computer Scientist and Director of Research at Google, Peter Norvig. Udacity© seeks to provide an online training experience for beginning, intermediate, and advanced technology skills. The programs range from 6 to 12 months in length depending upon the level of commitment a person makes when enrolling in the program. They seek to change the way people attain post-secondary education related to various "in-demand" technologies. On this site, they have created a "Nanodegree™" (Udacity) and they work with large corporate partners such as: AT&T, Google, Amazon, Adobe, Mercedes Benz, and many more. They offer technical training programs such as: "Robotics, Digital Marketing, Self-Driving Car Engineer, Virtual Reality Developer, Machine Learning Engineer, Data Analyst, Android Developer, iOs Developer, Front End Developer, Full Stack Developer" (Udacity) and many others. They offer this training along with job placement after the training is complete. The individuals that started Udacity© are fully aware of the high demand our country and the world will have for a technically-trained workforce. It will come down to the people who have "technical" skills being the ones that are most in demand moving forward into the mid-21st Century. Our middle, high school, and college students all need this information so they can acquire the differentiating skills that will set them apart and offer tremendous opportunity.

The other online training program that offers a great opportunity is https://skillcrush.com (Skillcrush). The program involves HTML5, CSS3, and JavaScript online training. Skillcrush© offers multiple training opportunities. On the https://skillcrush.com (Skillcrush) website, an explanation of the training programs that are offered is provided in the form of a "blueprint". They have "blueprints" for the following training options: "Freelance WordPress Developer, Visual Designer, Web Designer, Web Developer, Front End Developer, WordPress Bootcamp" (Skillcrush). I discovered https://skillcrush.com (Skillcrush) in May, 2016 so I signed up for their RSS (Real Simple Syndication) Feeds which enables me to receive updates from them almost daily. I make sure that all of my students know about these post-secondary options.

VIII. What Paths to Pursue Your Purpose

APPRENTICESHIPS......EARN WHILE YOU LEARN

For the student who is more of a "hands-on" learner, apprenticeships offer great opportunities. This is a structured, meaningful job training program that prepares a person for a career in the trades. An apprenticeship program will usually offer a 4-year training program with classroom and on the job training and actual work experience under an experienced, skilled expert. I attended a job fair at a career technical center a couple of years ago where representatives from apprenticeship programs also attended. I approached one of the apprenticeship representatives from the local Laborer's Union. I introduced myself and started asking questions about the Laborer's Apprenticeship. The representative quickly informed me about the great job opportunities that the Laborer's Union could offer. Then he proceeded to tell me about how he got into the job as a recruiter for them. I expressed interest in hearing his story. He told me that while he was attending a local state university he would work for the laborer's union on breaks from college and during his summers. So when he graduated from college with his Bachelor's Degree he could not find a full-time position in his major that would earn enough money for him to support himself.

He went back to work as a laborer for the union. Then a position opened up for a recruiter for the apprenticeship program and that's how he obtained the job as the Laborer's Union Apprenticeship Recruiter. What a great story of someone who was working while in college and used that connection to secure a full-time job with a living wage and benefits after college.

As I read about how other countries incorporate apprenticeship opportunities for their adolescents, I discovered that there are several European Countries that have successful apprenticeship programs that are offered between 9th and 10th grades, much like our career technical program offerings. However, in their systems, they incorporate apprenticeships into their training where students get actual work experience as they are learning. Finland and Denmark are the two countries that use the same time period that the American Educational System uses to channel their students toward career technical education programs. Students and their parents in Finland and Denmark are involved in the decision-making process to determine what apprenticeship opportunity would best fit the students' interests and aptitudes. In Germany, employers are very involved in this process as well. German employers are investing in the development of a young person's skills with hopes that the young person will invest their career within a company that made the investment of training, time, and attention. America needs to consider creating sustainable relationships between high schools and employers to better equip this new generation of workers to learn about the multitude of opportunities the 21st Century will offer.

Entering the Workforce after High School

After the pressures of completing all the standardized tests and academic rigor of high school, some students just want to go out and enter the workforce. Of course, it is an option that most parents may not support because they may think that their student may not go back to continue their post-secondary education. If a student chooses this option, the student should develop an action plan toward pursuing some kind of post-secondary training. From this experience, a student can develop an awareness and understanding of the free enterprise system and enable the student to earn and save some money. Both of these experiences will benefit the student's life. If the student does not have "career maturity" before leaving high school, they will gain "career maturity" through going to work. This can be a good experience and allow the student to formulate a plan without the pressure of completing the requirements of their high school credits.

Students complain about what teachers require of them to complete a high school class for the exchange of a high school credit toward graduation. The daily requirements of what a boss will require is an eye-opening experience for many youth in this generation. There is nothing that can replace the development or enhancement of a young person's work ethic to set a course for their work life. I know of a local business that is headquartered near where I live that hires young people while they are still in high school in order to provide opportunities for them to be promoted from within as they mature and display value in the business. I attended another career fair last year where a recruiter from this company attended. As I spoke to the recruiter, he explained the company's philosophy of hiring entry-level workers and what they would be offered in advancement opportunities.

I have to say that going from high school to work would be one of the quickest ways to acquire both emotional and career maturity. Many youth today do not have any job experience, volunteer work, or even community service that has enabled them to "grow up". As stated earlier, work provides many benefits and a byproduct of that experience is maturity.

Chapter IX
Our World Needs People with Technical Skills ..... Is This a Path For You to find Your Purpose?

Coding Skills as Part of the Core Curriculum?

We all know computers have become an integral part of every organization, corporation, small business, school, government agency, workplace, and non-profit. In other words, computers are part of everything we do! Information Technology, computer programming, computer science, and software development have changed the way we do things. Technology has enabled us to use a computer to:

1) Communicate
2) Learn
3) Travel

4) Shop
5) Socialize
6) Search for a job
7) Find a husband or wife
8) Visit with family and friends
9) Earn a College Degree
10) Get Access to Entertainment
   . . . . . . and much more!

These are all good things for the most part. Of course, there are things online that children should not be exposed to, but many children receive a smart phone by their 10th birthday so we are actually giving them access to the best and worst of the web right in their hands. My question is "Does a 10 year old have the cognitive skills to understand the capability of what a smart phone can do and how it can influence them?" Another consideration is the safety element of providing your child a phone at such a young age. Today's cell phones are not just phones; they are computers and we have to realize that we are exposing our children to unneeded radiation to their young brains. There is an increasing amount of research being done in this field that questions whether it is safe to allow a small child to put a smart phone to their head. Like everything, we have to decide what technologies our children should be given access to and what technologies can wait until they have developed

IX. Our World Needs People with Technical Skills...

an awareness of what is "appropriate" and what is "not appropriate". What a child sees, cannot be unseen by a child. Let's protect them as long as we can.

On another note regarding technology, I have been teaching coding skills (Hypertext Markup Language and Cascading Style Sheets) for over ten years and I have researched the topic of incorporating coding skills into the core curriculum. I must say I would agree that teaching coding skills as part of the academic core would be very beneficial to our K-12 students. From my experience, learning how to code engages and interests students. It grows confidence and attachment to a "real-world" skill that is very much in demand. When students are learning something that they are really interested in, they come to class, get to work, and stay engaged until the bell rings for the next class. It is awesome to see students who are excited to learn how to code.

First, I am in agreement with Hadi Partovi of https://code.org (Code) when he presented a Ted Talk© on "Computer Science is Foundational" (Computer Science is Foundational). He speaks about how learning computer science while in our K-12 school systems can prepare and equip our students to succeed in the 21st Century Marketplace. I could not agree more. We need to realize that our students will be engaged in information technology tasks in any career field they enter. Second, if our K-12 students are engaged in understanding computer science, programming languages, and coding skills, the better the chances are for them to succeed as they transition into college, technical school, and the 21st Century Workforce.

BENEFITS OF TEACHING CODING SKILLS AS PART OF THE CORE CURRICULUM

Students are interested in coding because they know that it is a 21st Century Skill that they can use in high school and beyond. Students are motivated to learn coding because they live "online" and want to understand how applications and websites work. Students like to solve problems and be creative. Learning coding skills promotes creativity, problem solving, and critical thinking. When students are learning coding skills, they have to think for themselves and solve the problem to make the code work. An application of this is when the student runs the code in their browser and the "code" doesn't work, the student has to refer back to the code, find the error, and correct it.

The non-profit, https://code.org (Code) focuses on providing online training opportunities for K-12 students to learn coding skills. This organization has collected the statistics from all fifty states on the number of job openings in the computer science field versus the number of qualified graduates in each state. Additionally, https://code.org (Code) seeks to help school districts implement training programs for K-12 teachers.

For the past three years, I have had my students participate in an "Hour of Code" (Code). The students have enjoyed this activity and after they complete their "Hour of Code" (Code) they receive a printed certificate from https://code.org (Code). Students with all ability levels have participated in this event (special needs, typical, and gifted). From this experience, I am confident in saying that all students, regardless of their ability level, have greatly benefitted from this experience.

Students are using technology for mostly social media, texting, applications, an occasional phone call, and web search capabilities. Students should not just be users of technology products; they should be creators of technology products. The younger generation tends to be among the most creative and innovative. There is much untapped potential in our students to create technology while they are in our K-12 school systems. We all know how quickly they learn and adapt to the technology.

What Coding Skills Can Offer a Student

As technology proliferates, our students will benefit from having an understanding of where all of this technology got started. If they learn how to code, learn how to design websites, and learn how to be lifelong learners, they will set themselves apart in the 21st Century Workforce. When students learn how to code, some of the outcomes will be: Development of creative abilities, problem solving, applying logical and computational thinking (which are all 21st Century In-Demand Skills). For all the students who gravitate toward the art courses in high school and college, learning how to code can be a way for a creative student to channel their gift sets. Once students have coding skills (in HTML5, CSS3, and JavaScript), they can create online content to make their own website.

As I begin the content of my coding class, I present a lesson on "Internet and Web History". Most students think that the "internet" and the "web" are the same thing. I review the history of the development of the "internet" and then the development of the "web". The lesson covers that the internet is much older than the web. I review historical dates when the internet was developed and who was involved in the development of ARPANET (Advanced Research Projects Agency Network) and TCP/IP (Transmission Control Protocol/Internet Protocol) as being the early components of what we know as the Internet. We also cover the development of the World Wide Web and they learn who invented this technology...Tim Berners-Lee. The students learn that the internet is about (hardware) and the web is about (software) and how people connect to this technology.

Then I begin to teach HTML5 (Hypertext Markup Language) and CSS3 (Cascading Style Sheets) to get some basic coding skills in place. With these two skills, the students can code a basic website and they learn how to transfer their HTML code and CSS stylesheet to a website that will publish their customized code. After this training, the students learn basic computer science principles and introduction to programming. By the end of the semester, the students are excited about what they have learned and I demonstrate websites where they can continue to work on their skills.

Having coding and an introduction to programming experience while still in high school gives students an advantage no matter where their post-secondary options take them beyond high school. Because we know that all parents want their children to be equipped to succeed in the 21st Century, these skills lay the groundwork toward that success. It is not about "going into computers" for a career field. All career fields will need people with these skills. I have observed students in an Introductory Coding Class to be focused, disciplined, and excited about what they are learning. Some students in this generation, are not engaged in classes with content they are not interested in learning; even though, those same classes are required to graduate. They will gravitate toward courses that will challenge them, engage them, and motivate them to learn 21st Century Skills. As this class is an elective, the students generally sign up for the class because of their interest in computers. This past year, these students have demonstrated their eagerness to learn, their attention to detail, and their excitement about gaining a 21st Century Skill. The students in the coding classes are concerned about making sure their code works as they "run" the code in a browser.

Additionally, when students learn how to code and have an understanding of computer science, students can use their creative abilities, develop collaborative skills (working in teams), and solve problems. All of those skills can transfer into other classes as well as to a person's work life. I have seen students be very diligent and persistent to correct their code error and get the website to run properly. All of these skills are valuable to the 21st Century Workforce or an Entrepreneurial Endeavor students may pursue.

Technology Proliferates

But you, Daniel, keep this prophecy a secret; seal up the book until the time of the end, when many will rush here and there, and knowledge will increase.
Daniel 12:4

Many Biblical Scholars have debated the issue that technology continuing to evolve refers to what was mentioned in the Book of Daniel. Our busy lifestyles today do involve us rushing around. Years ago, people did not fly as much as they do today. In most homes, both parents are working full-time to sustain the family's lifestyle. Our work days are long and children are involved in various after-school and extracurricular activities. Technology has offered us ways to improve our lives as technology continues to evolve.

Our challenge is as technology evolves, we must remember that human interaction and the development of human relationships will never be replaced by anything we do on our computers, tablets, or phones. This generation will see technology proliferating at a faster speed than any other generation. We need to make sure they know how to properly interact, interview, and communicate with people in authority over them, with co-workers, and customers.

CHAPTER X
Career Paths in the 21st Century

CAREER CLUSTERS – A STARTING PLACE FOR STUDENTS

In the late 1990s, the Department of Education working with other career and technical education initiatives developed 16 career clusters. The National Career Clusters® (Career Clusters…) are identified in the following categories:

1. Agriculture, Food, and Natural Resources
2. Architecture & Construction
3. Arts, A/V Technology & Communication
4. Business Management & Administration
5. Education & Training
6. Finance
7. Government & Public Administration
8. Health Sciences
9. Hospitality & Tourism

10. Human Services
11. Information Technology
12. Law, Public Safety, Corrections, & Security
13. Manufacturing
14. Marketing
15. STEM (Science, Technology, Engineering & Mathematics)
16. Transportation, Distribution, & Logistics (Career Clusters...)

These categories are broad, but they can help students focus on specific interests and eliminate categories that are not interesting to them at all. When students enter 8th grade, this may be an optimal time to offer a survey of these categories to them and again in 9th and 10th grades. Documentation of these surveys can be a component of the career portfolio. Other components of a career portfolio could be the following:

1. Personality Type
2. Values
3. Learning Style
4. Strengths
5. Work Preferences
6. Resume
7. Goal/Personal Statement
8. Cover Letter
9. Computer Skills

X. Career Paths in the 21st Century

Helping our students identify career clusters that interest them and providing guidance to the students should be a priority during their high school experience. Upon entry into high school or even during 8th grade, students should participate in interest surveys throughout their time in these grades to target career clusters. Career Exploration lessons can be incorporated into most classes with intention from the teacher. From my experience, students are really interested in learning about careers and they also enjoy learning about "real world" topics. I believe more "real world" lessons should be addressed in high school to equip and prepare them for the realities of college and the world of work. The American Workforce needs new workers with a "strong work ethic". So often when newly graduated students transition into the workforce either in part-time or full-time work, they have a huge learning curve to adapt to the 21st Century workplace. I believe that if students are provided opportunity to develop a career development portfolio from the end of middle school to the end of high school, students would have a "starting point" in connecting to an appropriate major toward a career cluster that most interests them. When students have a starting point in a career path, they are more motivated to succeed in high school because they have a goal to work toward, not just the high school diploma.

Career and Technical Education on the Rise

When a high school student has an opportunity to attend a career and technical training program in high school, this is not the 20th Century "Vo-Tech" Training that most parents would not want their child to attend. Our Career Technical Programs during high school are preparing students for in-demand 21st Century "real-world" opportunities. Just like college is not for everyone, career technical training is not for everyone. I understand this option as a way to teach "hands-on" skills to a student who is kinesthetic in their learning style. Toward the end of the career technical training, usually during senior year, a student is offered work opportunities through the school's cooperative education coordinator. The cooperative education coordinator is responsible for connecting students who have received training to local employers who have a labor need for the training the students have received. Cooperative education coordinators have credentials that prove they have an understanding and application of the federal and state child labor laws. When a career technical student has the opportunity to go to work while still in high school, I have seen this experience do several things for the student.

X. Career Paths in the 21st Century

A student can experience the follow:

1) Gain Career Maturity
2) Earn Money
3) Gain Practical Work Experience in their Career Technical Field
4) Contribute to the Economy
5) Gain Soft Skills and Employability Skills
6) A Possible Full-Time Job Opportunity after Graduation

If a student chooses to go to a 4-year college after career technical training, all of those skills and experiences, go with the student. Therefore, career technical training can serve as an advantage for the student as they develop a career path. Those career technical skills can be used while the student is in college to earn a higher income than a retail or food service job.

As discussed in an earlier chapter, by the end of 9th grade, a student should be able to make the decision whether they are on the college-bound track or the career/technical training track. If a student is interested in the career/technical track, pursuing this opportunity while still in high school is the optimal time for training. The training is relevant and it is available without paying tuition. However, one of the hindrances to a student attending career technical training during high school may be a lack of career maturity or a lack of awareness of career and technical fields that are in demand.

Career and Technical Education is not what it used to be. The 21st Century has changed everything. This table, presented in Edmentum's White Paper entitled: *"Career & Technical Education: How Are You Addressing the Growing Need?"* (Auger 3), illustrates how career and technical education has changed in the 21st Century:

CTE Historically	CTE Now
Designed for High School	Designed to Bridge the Link Between High School & Postsecondary Education
6-7 Program Areas	16 Clusters 70 Career Paths
Not Standardized	Common Career & Technical Core Standards
Non-Academically Oriented	Supports and Reinforces Academic Learning
Ends at High School	Continual Opportunities for Stackable Certificates & Degrees

Source: Auger, Jasmine. Edmentum White Paper, Career & Technical Education: How are you addressing the growing need? June, 2015, page 3.

X. Career Paths in the 21st Century

Career and Technical fields are growing because of the large amount of baby boomers who are and will continue to retire. Millennials will have abundant opportunities to find and fulfill their purposes, but they will still have to compete to enter the workforce and advance in the workforce. I recently received an e-mail from the area high school where I live about a career awareness night being offered to students, parents, and teachers as an evening program about the multitude of career technical jobs that will be available by 2020 in Pennsylvania. The program involved a presentation on specialized career fields in the areas of manufacturing, healthcare, energy, transportation, information technology, and the skilled trade fields. The presentation sought to help students, parents, and teachers change their 20th Century assumptions about Career Technical Fields. It is time for parents and students to have an understanding and awareness of how these Career Technical Opportunities can be achieved with an Associate's Degree to obtain a family-sustaining wage.

21ST CENTURY LABOR MARKET — WHAT ARE EMPLOYERS SEEKING?

As mentioned earlier, the 21st Century is very different from the 20th Century. Technology and the way we work has changed everything. In 2008, when the bottom dropped out of the economy, employers have changed the way they hire people.

A Non-Profit organization in Bethlehem, PA, the National Association of Colleges and Employers, has conducted research on the skills employers are seeking in new hires. These attributes are listed with the highest ranking to the lowest ranking:

1. Leadership
2. Ability to Work in a Team
3. Communication Skills (written)
4. Problem Solving
5. Strong Work Ethic
6. Analytical/Quantitative Skills
7. Technical Skills
8. Communication Skills (verbal)
9. Initiative
10. Computer Skills
11. Flexibility/Adaptability
12. Interpersonal Skills (relates well to others)
13. Detail-Oriented
14. Organizational Ability
15. Strategic Planning Skills
16. Friendly/Outgoing Personality
17. Entrepreneurial Skills/Risk-Taker
18. Tactfulness
19. Creativity (Gray and Koncz)

As I reviewed this paper on what employers want in new college hires, I realized that the majority of these skills (with one exception, Strategic Planning Skills) can and should be taught in middle and high school and strengthened and further developed and enhanced in college. With this insight from the National Association of Colleges and Employers, middle and high school teachers could be very instrumental in the development of these skill sets so that after the student completes a post-secondary experience, they would be entering the workforce with all of these skills in place. Unfortunately, there is evidence this is not currently happening. From a White Paper (a research paper) from Lynda.com, *"College and Workplace Readiness: Preparing Students for the Future with Online Instruction"* (Lynda.com), reports:

> **"Students aren't graduating from high school and entering the workplace or college with the right blend of skills they need for success"** (Lynda.com).

These skills are critical to a student's successfully transitioning into college or the workplace. Middle and high school teachers can play an integral part in the development and enhancement of the above-mentioned skills. After the student graduates, the skills will transfer wherever the student goes. Additionally, Lynda.

com's White Paper, *"College and Workplace Readiness: Preparing Students for the Future with Online Instruction"* (Lynda.com) reveals insight on what employers are seeking:

> "Employers want incoming workers to possess a core set of soft skills that includes critical thinking, communication, creativity, innovation, problem solving, and collaboration" (Lynda.com).

All of these soft skills are teachable in elementary, middle and high school. It's time to link what we are doing in the K-12 systems to what the workforce needs. There should be a direct correlation to what we are doing in schools to prepare this next generation for the realistic demands of the 21st Century Workforce.

These skills can be incorporated in middle and high school by the way we deliver instruction and engage students in the classroom. As I mentioned in an earlier chapter, I strongly believe in Project-Based Learning. Students are given a problem, instruction on problem solving, provided resources, and given a specific period of time to solve the problem. Many soft skills are developed, utilized, and enhanced during this process. The country of Finland has experienced much success within their educational systems. I recently read a quote from an article entitled, *"Why Are Finland's Schools So Successful?"* (Hancock) that really spoke to me. It was a quote from Kari Louhivuori, the principal from Kirkkojarvi Comprehensive School, that said:

> **"This is what we do every day, prepare kids for life" (Hancock).**

This is why I believe the United States should be interested in learning about how Finland has experienced such success with their public school systems.

Chapter XI
People Skills/Soft Skills..... God Wants Us To Relate Well with One Another

Why People Skills/Soft Skills are Necessary for a Student to Succeed

God blesses those who work for peace,
for they will be called the children of God.
Matthew 5:9

In the same way, you who are younger
must accept the authority of the elders.
And all of you, dress yourselves in
humility as you relate to one another, for
"God opposes the proud
but gives grace to the humble."
1 Peter 5:5

> *A gentle answer deflects anger,*
> *but harsh words make tempers flare.*
>
> **Proverbs 15:1**

As the Bible directs and guides us how to relate and interact appropriately with our fellow man, we should be concerned about how we are teaching this next generation to communicate effectively with one another. As they are emerging into the workforce, many of them do not have the appropriate "soft skills" to successfully integrate into their adult lives as full-time workers. By "soft skills", I mean a variety of things: Communication, Interpersonal Skills, Problem Solving, Conflict Resolution, Time Management, Organizational Acumen, and a Strong Work Ethic. These are just a few of the "soft skills" newly-hired workers (both out of high school and out of college) will need to improve on to become productive in our companies, organizations, start-ups, and government agencies. In reflecting on why this generation needs to improve on these very important skills for workplace success, their use of social media, texting, and technology as a whole are the primary drivers of the deficiencies in their development and sometimes inappropriate application of "soft skills". They are not getting enough practice as previous generations did because the previous generations did

XI. People Skills/Soft Skills....

not have the technology available. We were provided opportunities along the way to develop and enhance these very essential, critical skills without technology. In other words, we had to develop face-to-face skills.

Healthy relationships are the cornerstone to healthy living. The better our communication skills are the better our relationships with people at work, at home, at church, and in our communities will be. God is the Creator of relationships and His Word provides much on communicating effectively with others.

People who are entering the workforce would benefit from being mindful that these human relation skills are essential and critical within an organization. Young people can enhance these skills by intentionally being involved in experiences, opportunities, and educational enrichment programs that provide development of "soft skills". Work (whether it is paid or voluntary) is probably the best vehicle to improve and enhance these "soft skills". However, when these skills are developed in a workplace, reduced productivity or financial loss may be the result of a deficiency of these skills. Employers are not in the business of providing basic training of these essential skills, but they are affected by the lack of these skills by low productivity rates and high turnover rates.

Extracurricular opportunities that students can involve themselves in may be a great vehicle for the development and enhancement of these skills. Being involved in student organizations while in high school or college provide opportunities for students to develop a variety of skills. Some of them include: Leadership, Troubleshooting, Diplomacy, Open-mindedness, Humility, Interpersonal Skills, Cultural Sensitivity, Diversity Awareness, Public Speaking, Collaboration (Teamwork), Conflict Resolution, and Communication (improved Reading, Writing, Listening, and Speaking) Skills. Students should get involved in extracurricular activities as soon as they enter high school. I believe sports teams are good vehicles for extracurricular involvement; however, I highly recommend active involvement in other opportunities as well. Students will benefit from early involvement in extracurricular activities, i.e. when applying for scholarships, their involvement matters.

Educational Enrichment Programs that offer students opportunities and experiences to develop and enhance these skills are offered through a wide variety of venues while students are in high school and college: Summer programs, camps, youth conventions, university outreach programs, sport teams, specialty training programs offered by technical schools, adult education programs, and community college non-credit programs to name a few. Development of these critical, essential skills while in high school will help the student set themselves apart.

XI. People Skills/Soft Skills....

If only high school students were aware of how important these skills are to their future success, they would be involved in every organization possible while in high school. For the students in this generation who have or are working on developing and enhancing these skills, they will take on leadership positions earlier if they are cognizant of how much these skills are in demand and needed in the workforce.

SOCIAL MEDIA: BEING APPROPRIATE

Because Social Media is so ingrained in our society today, students need to have a proper awareness of how the application of social media will affect their future personal, work, and social lives. Parents should caution what their teens are doing on social media to properly protect them from a sin-stained world. We know that some students in this generation think nothing of posting a photo, video, or text of something that is not appropriate. It takes time to teach and train a child on what is "appropriate". The world, the flesh, and the devil have stacked the deck against us as parents by making things so readily available to our children. Our children are overwhelmed with images, videos, posts, texting, and technology to the point that we have lost some of these precious children to suicide. How can the situation be so horrible that a teen even thinks about or considers this option? Our teens need to know who God is and what God has done for them through Jesus.

> *God saved you by his grace*
> *when you believed.*
> *And you can't take credit for this;*
> *it is a gift from God.*
> Ephesians 2:8

> *For since our friendship with God was restored by the death of his Son while we were still his enemies, we will certainly be saved through the life of his Son.*
> Romans 5:10

DEVELOP YOURSELF (GRACIOUSLY)

Our teens need help to develop themselves with grace, dignity, and self-awareness so that they may be able to successfully transition into post-secondary opportunities and the 21st Century Workforce. One of the textbooks I have used in teaching career development for teens is *"Becoming the Best Me: 10 Career and Character Education Essentials"*, by Dr. Robert Orndorff.

He conducted research on what qualities employers in the 21st Century are seeking. Based on Dr. Orndorff's research, he found that the following attributes were the "essentials":

1) Become a People Person
2) Appreciate Diversity
3) Become a Team Player
4) Become a Person of Character
5) Communicate Effectively
6) Become Computer Proficient
7) Pay Attention to the Right Things
8) Become a Leader
9) Connect to the World Around You
10) Become an Active Explorer (Orndorff 1)

I agree all of these attributes are "essentials" for the workforce. Our challenge in the public school systems is to incorporate opportunities for students to gain not just awareness of these attributes, but gain experience in these areas.

When students, parents, and teachers intentionally work together to develop academic skills and character development, we are addressing the "whole" person. As a student enters high school, parents are the critical component to that student's success in the four years they spend there. As we all know, much change happens from 9th to 12th Grade. The emotional support that high school students receive from their parents during this time can be life changing or even life saving. Parents should never underestimate how important they are to their teenagers. If we want them to develop (graciously), we must show them what graciousness is by our examples, our behavior, and our language. We must also remember we are teaching them how to be parents themselves someday.

> *Fathers, do not provoke your children to anger by the way you treat them. Rather, bring them up with the discipline and instruction that comes from the Lord.*
> *Ephesians 6:4*

> *Discipline your children, and they will give you peace of mind and will make your heart glad.*
> *Proverbs 29:17*

> *Don't use foul or abusive language. Let everything you say be good and helpful, so that your words will be an encouragement to those who hear them.*
> *Ephesians 4:29*

XI. People Skills/Soft Skills....

TEENS NEED NURTURING, TOO!

All too often when a student enters high school, we tend to think that they are almost "grown". During a teen's years in high school, they have much to learn and to experience to properly matriculate into adulthood. Through working with teens in different settings, I have observed many of them who need much encouragement and support. I want to encourage parents for a moment here. Parents are busy, responsible people with so much on their plates. Parents need their children and children need their parents to guide them through the transitions of adolescence into adulthood. When a teen has a bad day, they might just come home and immerse themselves in social media instead of talking out the problem with a caring parent. When a teen is depressed, starts using drugs, and changes friend groups, these are all signs that the teen really needs to connect with their parent. When our children are small and young, it is easy and natural to nurture them. God wants us to nurture and care for teens because they need that support when they are experiencing so much change (physically, emotionally, and mentally). I realize that this is a time when teens want to begin to establish themselves as independent of their parents. Many teens are making choices without regard to parental input and some of those choices are leading down a path of destruction. We as parents have to find a middle ground between hovering over this generation and being "hands-off" when teens are making bad decisions and choices. We need to remember that our teenagers need our involvement, encouragement, patience, intervention, and guidance as we help them navigate their way into becoming an adult in our complex world.

> *Don't worry about anything; instead,*
> *pray about everything. Tell God what you*
> *need, and thank him for all he has done.*
> *Philippians 4:6*

Many teens have fear transitioning out of high school and entering the next phase of their lives. When I speak with a teen who expresses fear, I try to speak with them about what they are afraid of "specifically". This fear is rooted in anxiety of the unknown. I have seen the anxiety reduced when a student takes time to properly assess themselves, explore careers, and develop a beginning career path as they transition out of high school. This generation needs to know how much our country needs them to be trained, equipped, and ready for the demands of the 21st Century Workforce.

XI. People Skills/Soft Skills....

Our young people need to be aware of this scripture. If they are aware of this scripture and apply it to their lives, the fear and anxiety of the unknown after high school or after college would be eliminated. The enemy of their souls wants them to be filled with fear and anxiety so he can hinder them from finding God's Plan and Purpose for their lives. We as parents need to take hold of this ourselves and not be hindered by anxiety and fear in our own lives so we can guide our children toward what God has purposed them to do.

In the last school year, I was teaching a class where one of the subjects was "Going on a Job Interview". After we finished the lesson, I decided to do mock interviews with a few of the students. I provided them some mock interview questions and I set the scenario up in the classroom. After we finished the mock interview, I would critique the interview by providing positive feedback to the student and constructive feedback on what they could improve upon for an actual interview. As I was reviewing my notes, one senior in the class spoke up in a timid voice, but we all heard him. He said, "I am scared." Then another senior said, "I am scared too." I had known both of these students since freshmen year so when I heard them say they were both scared, I stopped reviewing the mock interview. I asked them why they were scared. They both explained their reasons.

Sometimes we see these adult size bodies and think they can handle things like an adult, but many of them are scared. Parents, I want to encourage you to continue to nurture, encourage, and support your adolescent.

CHAPTER XII
When a Child Knows His or Her Purpose....

THE ADVANTAGED LIFE

Children that are brought up knowing and accepting God's Truths from when they are young will have advantages over children who are not taught or do not know or accept God's Truths. For with God, a person always has advantages. Ted Shuttlesworth, Jr. has a quote in his book, *"Blood on the Door: The Power of Protective Covenant"* about how God has purposed every child. Ted writes about a quote from his grandfather: "You are not an accident, you were created by divine design. You are unique and your purpose has been tailor-made just for you" (Shuttlesworth 42). The Shuttlesworth Family has raised their children in the fear and admonition of the Lord and the children were trained to know what it means to live in the Full Authority of what Jesus has done for us. The Shuttlesworth Family has produced several amazing evangelists who hold meetings where signs and wonders are demonstrated through the Power of the Holy Ghost. I have been in several of Jonathan Shuttlesworth's meetings when he refers to using your gifts when considering a career. I have to say that Jonathan and Ted are fully aware of their gifts and they use them to glorify God in their Ministries.

The outcome of being raised under these circumstances has a life-changing effect on a person that will impact all their days. Jesus came to provide abundant life. We have health, wholeness, prosperity, peace, love, self-control, safety, blessings, and the list goes on. What a life He has purchased for us on Calvary's Cross! His desire is that all people know what was purchased for them, receive Him as Lord and Savior, and walk in the Full Authority of being redeemed. God wants to move in your life and your child's life. All you have to do is surrender to Him and seek Him daily!

Personality Types: Why Knowing Your Type Can Provide Insight

God has ordained your child's personality. When a child (let's say a middle school-aged student), knows their personality it provides much insight for the child. It helps a student to get to know their traits and it gives them time to understand those traits as they work their way through the middle and high school years. When a

XII. When a Child Knows His or Her Purpose. . . . .

student knows their personality, it builds confidence in that student. Additionally, when a student knows these traits, they can engage in academic and extracurricular activities where those traits can be developed, enhanced, and utilized. It is a beginning of self-understanding when done early in life. Many adults have never learned their personality type.

I work with students in primarily business and/or computer classes; however, I do make time to assess personality traits of all of my students at the beginning of the semester because it helps me to understand the traits that the students possess. I find it helpful to know if a student is an Extrovert or an Introvert, whether the student is a dominant Thinker or dominant Feeling Person. After they take a personality test, I show the students how to look up information on their personalities. They are always amazed at how accurate the personality descriptions match the qualities they possess. They are usually fascinated when they are reading about their personality profiles. Another part of this assignment is for them to research what careers are suggested for whatever personality type they are. It gives them a starting place to understand how their personality type may match with a potential career. I tell them the story about when I was in college and discovered am I an ESFJ® (Extravert Sensing Feeling

Judging)® from the Jung Typology Test™. I learned that ESFJs® are good in the fields of business or education. I tell the students that I combined the fields of business and education and became a business teacher and how this career was a right fit for me. Because the work I do is toward "my bent" (in keeping with my "personal gifts") it does not feel like work. I want all of my students to identify their personality type and learn how to choose a career that utilizes their "personal gifts". It is important to have this information about yourself when you are young. I record the personality type information and ask them to keep track of it for future reference. I say to the students, "You know your shoe size; you should know your personality type!" Knowing your personality type and how personality types affect human interaction, not only helps you understand yourself, but it also helps you learn how to appreciate other personality types in your home, your school, and your workplace. This is valuable information as a person transitions from high school to post-secondary endeavors.

XII. When a Child Knows His or Her Purpose. . . . .

WHAT GOD WANTS FOR YOU . . . . . .

Because Jesus has already died and rose again to save people from their sins, He has done everything for us to be reconciled to Him. Now our part is to receive what Jesus has done for us. The problem comes in when our hearts are full of rebellion. God wants to be involved in every decision, every small, trivial thing and every large, monumental thing in our lives. He wants us to be aware of His Presence in our lives. He wants us to seek His Counsel in everything. The Holy Spirit will suggest, guide, and illuminate answers to us as we seek Him and stay connected to Him.

So this is the advantaged life! Will you claim it for yourself and your child? Jesus is waiting to pour out His Blessings on Your Life and Your Child's Life.

We have a choice to make every day and here is the choice:

Will You Live in the Blessings of Obedience or the Curses of Disobedience?

I know which one I will choose!

One of my favorite worship groups to listen to hails from the Elevation Church in North Carolina. In their song, "Yahweh", I love this quote from the song:

> "Each person's life is but breath, unending promise. God's Divine Breath flows through You and those around You. Heaven inside us when you breathe, you let God in, whispers the sound of your Name. Jesus called out with a loud voice" **(Elevation Worship).**
>
> *('Father into Your Hands I commit my Spirit.')*
> **Luke 23:46**

This is what we are in Him!
Knowing this, changes everything!

Concluding Thoughts

As Jesus died a sinner's death on Calvary's Cross for you and me, his last breath offers us our first breath into eternity when we receive Him as Personal Lord and Savior. It is truly that simple. We are **not saved** by our **morality, good works, religion,** or **anything we can do to earn our way**. If we could earn our way, why then did Jesus die a criminal's death when He was not a criminal? It is His Shed Blood that can make us right with God, nothing we can or ever will do changes that. Knowing that I know this, humbles me to receive what Jesus has done for me that I cannot do for myself. It is about having

XII. When a Child Knows His or Her Purpose. . . . .

a personal relationship with the Lord of Lords and the King of Kings. What sacrifice He made to have us spend eternity with Him?

Our purpose is to discover what God has created us to accomplish for the life He gave us. I pray this book brings your child closer to finding what God has purposed them to accomplish, achieve, and attain because they are the only one that can fulfill God's Plans for their lives.

Blessings overflow to
you and your family!

Assessment Citations

Jung Typology Test™ (Carl Jung's and Isabel Briggs Myers Typological Approach) 1998-2017 Human Metrics, Human Metrics, Inc., www.humanmetrics.com Accessed 10 Oct. 2016, www.humanmetrics.com/personality

CareerPerfect® – Free Career Planning Tests, Career Perfect – Our Difference, Your Advantage, www.careerperfect.com 1996-2017 CareerPerfect.com is the online Division of Career Services Group, Inc. Accessed 5 Nov. 2016, https://www.careerperfect.com/tips/career-planning/free-tests/

Minnesota State CAREERwise Education, Minnesota State Colleges and Universities, https://www.careerwise.mnscu.edu 2017 A Minnesota State Career and Education Resource, Accessed 4 Dec. 2016 https://www.careerwise.mnscu.edu/careers/assessyourself.html

Guidance Division Survey, Oklahoma Department of Career and Technology, 2005 https://cte.careertech.org/sites/default/files/StudentInterestSurvey-English.pdf Accessed 18 Feb. 2017.

What Career is Right for Me? Lean Up, LLC, 2016 www.whatcareerisrightforme.com/career-aptitude-test.php, Accessed 3 Mar. 2017.

Personal Values Assessment (PVA), Barrett Values Centre, 2016, www.valuescentre.com/our-products/products-individuals/personal-values-assessment-pva, Accessed 26 Feb. 2017.

Richard Step – Enrich Yourself & Step Up Your Career, Richard Step, 2017, http://richardstep.com/richardstep-strengths-weaknesses-aptitude-test/ Accessed 16 Mar. 2017.

Clifton Strengths, The Gallup Organization, 2017, https://www.gallupstrengthscenter.com/Home/en-US/Index/ Accessed 16 Aug. 2017.

Aptitude-Test.com, Seliant ApS, 2012, www.aptitude-test.com Accessed 17 Jan. 2017.

Education Planner, Pennsylvania Higher Education Assistance Agency, 2011, www.educationplanner.org Accessed 3 Mar. 2017.

Pennsylvania Career Zone, Pennsylvania Department of Education, 2011 www.pacareerzone.org Accessed 16 Apr. 2017.

XII. When a Child Knows His or Her Purpose. . . . .

Quick and Honest, GiftsTest.com in Partnership with BeliefNet, 2017, www.giftstest.com/test Accessed 7 Jun. 2017.

References

CHAPTER 2

Hagin, Kenneth. *The Untapped Power of Praise*, Broken Arrow, OK, RHEMA Bible Church, AKA Kenneth Hagin Ministries, Inc. 1990, page 105.

Buckingham, Marcus. *Trombone Player Wanted. YouTube.* YouTube, 24 Mar. 2015, Accessed 26 Dec. 2016.

CHAPTER 3

Clifton Strengths, The Gallup Organization, 2017. https://www.gallupstrengthscenter.com/Home/en-US/Index/ Accessed 16 Aug. 2017.

Judge, Timothy and Hurst, Charlice. *"How the Rich (and Happy) Get Richer (and Happier): Relationship of Core Self-Evaluations to Trajectories in Attaining Work Success."* Journal of Applied Psychology, University of Florida, vol. 93, 2008, page 849-863.

CHAPTER 4

Hovind, Chad. *"How to Delight in Your Children by Recognizing their God-Given Bend."* BeliefNet: Inspire Your Everyday, September 2011, http://www.beliefnet.com/columnists/godonomics/2011/09/how-to-delight-in-your-children-by-recognizing-their-god-given-bend.html. Accessed 20 Jun. 2017.

United States Congress, *"Exploring Careers: The ASVAB Career Exploration Guide"* DD Form 1304-5WB, Department of Defense, 2017, pages 5-17.

Bridging the Soft Skills Gap: Employers and New Hires Agree Soft Skills are Critical, but their Views on Preparedness are in Stark Contrast. Campos Research Strategy, Pittsburgh, PA, 2015, page 3, A report published by the Allegheny Conference on Community Development and the U.S. Chamber of Commerce Foundation.

Chapter 5
Bureau of Labor Statistics, *U.S. Current Population Survey: 2.5 Million Teens Out of Work of Unemployed,* 2013, Figure 2, Accessed 3 Mar. 2017.

Steinberg, Sarah Ayres. *America's 10 Million Unemployed Youth Spell Danger for Future Economic Growth* https://www.americanprogress.org/issues/economy/reports/2013/06/05/65373/americas-10million-unemployed-youth-spell-danger-for-future-economic-growth Accessed 14 Nov. 2016.

American Gap Association – Integrity in Gap Years, American Gap Association, 2017, Accessed 12 May 2017.

O'Shea, Joseph. *Gap Year: How Delaying College Changes People in Ways the World Needs,* Baltimore, MD, John Hopkins University Press, 2014, pages 2, 14, 24, 26, 27, 28, 29, 30, 33, 34.

Gray, Kenneth Dr. *Getting Real: Helping Teens Find their Future,* Thousand Oaks, CA, Corwin Press (A Sage Company), 2009, page 8.

Chapter 6
Phillips, Don. *The Hiram Code: Discovering the Ancient Secrets for Favor in the Last Days,* Lake Mary, FL, Charisma House, 2011, page 19.

Gray, Kenneth Dr. *Getting Real: Helping Teens Find their Future,* Thousand Oaks, CA, Corwin Press (A Sage Company), 2009, page 109.

The Chronicle of Higher Education College Completion, The Chronicle of Higher Education, 2017, www.collegecompletion.chronicle.com Pennsylvania College Completion Rates – Public University System – 4 and 6 year graduation rates, Accessed 3 Jun. 2017.

References

Chapter 7

Gray, Kenneth Dr. *Getting Real: Helping Teens Find Their Future,* Thousand Oaks, CA, Corwin Press (A Sage Company), 2009, page 70.

Walters, Genevra Dr. *"The Path to a STEM Job Starts in Elementary School: A Forward Thinking Superintendent Details How She Transformed Her General Education Program into a Series of Career Academies."* Scholastic Editor, Feb. 23, 2016, Accessed 25 Jan. 2017.

Symonds, W., et al. *Pathways to Prosperity: Meeting the Challenge of Preparing Young Americans for the 21st Century.* Harvard University Graduate School of Education, Cambridge, MA, 2011, page 3.

Jordan, Ann, and Crews, Tena. *Investigating Your Career,* Third Edition, Mason, OH, South-Western Cengage Learning, 2013, page 109.

Chapter 8

NOCTI, NOCTI, 2017, www.nocti.org/Blueprint.cfm, Accessed 3 Mar. 2017

SkillsUSA, SkillsUSA Inc., 2017 https://www.skillsusa.org/competitions/ Accessed 6 Apr. 2017.

Horn, L., and Berger, R. *"College Persistence on the Rise? Changes in 5-Year Degree Completion and Postsecondary Persistence Rates Between 1994-2000."* National Association of Student Personnel Administrators Journal, vol. 45, no. 3, 2005, Accessed 17 Apr. 2017.

Symonds, W., et al. *Pathways to Prosperity: Meeting the Challenge of Preparing Young Americans for the 21st Century,* Harvard University Graduate School of Education, Cambridge, MA, 2011, page 3.

United States Congress, *"Exploring Careers: The ASVAB Career Exploration Guide"* DD Form 1304-5WB, Department of Defense, 2017, pages 5-17

"What are Holland Codes? What is RIASEC?" *Career Key*, Career Key, Inc., 1987-2017, www.careerkey.org/choose-a-career/holland-codes-riasec.html#. Accessed 3 Jun 2017.

Udacity Nanodegree, Udacity, Inc., 2011, https://www.udacity.com. Accessed 2 Feb. 2017.

Skillcrush, Skillcrush, Inc., 2017 https://skillcrush.com. Accessed 14 Nov. 2016.

CHAPTER 9

Partovi, Hadi. "*Computer Science is Foundational*" *TEDxTalks* uploaded YouTube 10 Dec. 2014, Accessed 5 Mar. 2017.

Code, https://code.org, 2017, Accessed 15 May 2017.

CHAPTER 10

Pathways to College and Career Readiness Career Clusters, Advance CTE State Leaders Connecting Learning to Work, 2017, https://careertech.org/career-clusters. Accessed 16 Jun. 2017.

Clifton Strengths, The Gallup Organization, 2017. https://www.gallupstrengthscenter.com/Home/en-US/Index/ Accessed 12 Mar. 2017.

Auger, Jasmine. *Career & Technical Education: How Are You Addressing the Growing Need?* Edmentum White Paper, Bloomington, MN, 2015, page 3.

Gray, Kevin and Koncz, Andrea. *Job Outlook 2015: The Skills/ Qualities Employers Want in New College Graduate Hires*, National Association of Colleges and Employers, Bethlehem, PA, 2015.

Lynda.com. *College and Workplace Readiness: Preparing Students for the Future with Online Instruction.* North American Headquarters White Paper, Carpinteria, CA, 2015, page 2.

Hancock, Lynnell. *Why are Finland's Schools so Successful?* Smithsonian Magazine, September, 2011, www.smithsonianmag.com/innovation/why-are-finlands-schools-successful-49859555/. Accessed 3 Apr. 2017.

References

CHAPTER 11

Orndorff, Robert. *Becoming the Best Me: 10 Career and Character Education Essentials,* Indianapolis, IN, JIST Life, 2004, pages 1, 15, 29, 41, 57, 71, 87, 105, 121, 135.

CHAPTER 12

Shuttlesworth, Ted Jr. *Blood on the Door: The Protective Power of Covenant,* Virginia Beach, VA, Miracle Word Publishing, 2016, page 42.

Kwame. *Yahweh.* Elevation Worship at Elevation Church, NewReleaseToday, Charlotte, NC, 2016.

www.ingramcontent.com/pod-product-compliance
Lightning Source LLC
Chambersburg PA
CBHW071608170426
43196CB00034B/2229